HOW COME — MY FAITH?

MONKS OF MT. TABOR

how come my faith?

SOME WORDS ABOUT THE MEANING OF THE WORLD

bede reynolds, osb

ALBA BOOKS

CANFIELD, OHIO 44406

Imprimi Potest

+ Eugene Medved, O.S.B.
Abbot
Westminster Abbey,
Mission, B.C.
November 1973

Nihil Obstat

Daniel Carey
Censor Liborum

Imprimatur

James F. Carney, D.D.
Archbishop of Vancouver
November 19th, 1973

Library of Congress Catalog Card Number: 73-20883

ISBN: 0-8189-1117-4

Third Paperback Printing, June 1980.

Copyright © 1974 by

ALBA HOUSE COMMUNICATIONS
Canfield, Ohio 44406

TO OUR LADY
HELP OF CHRISTIANS – QUEEN OF ANGELS

MAY SHE
"Direct and order all my
doings in accordance with the
will of her only Son"

THANKS FOR EDITING

ARE DUE TO

SISTER MARY IMMACULATA, F.S.P.A.

MISS LYN MORROW

CONTENTS

FOREWORD

There can be little doubt that the Roman Catholic Church is entering the year 1974 in a state of grave spiritual crisis. There are thousands of indications of this, some tiny and trifling, some momentous and grave. Perhaps the most distressing of all of these indications is the devastating loss of confidence and stability among the clergy and religious of the whole Church. Coupled with this, and caused by it, is a woeful shortage of vocations among the young and a sense of distress and doubt and anxiety among the faithful in general.

The multitude of changes that have occurred during the past decade definitely reflect these conditions in the souls of men. The nature of some of these changes reflects in some degree a lessening of loyalty in the hearts of those from whom they stem.

The trend of many of the changes that have come about is toward a diminution of reverence and a lessening of dignity of expression. And through it all there is a diminution of respect and loyalty to the Holy Father.

The chapters that follow are written with the definite conviction that the vast majority of the six hundred million members of the Catholic laity have a longing for a return of reverence; a return of utter confidence in the assurance that the Promises of Christ still hold and that God has not altered the meaning of His words to Peter: "I also tell thee that thou art a rock and upon this rock I will build My Church, and the gates of hell shall not prevail against it." (Matt. 16:18).

How is it, then, that so much of what has occurred since the close of VATICAN II has seemed to contradict that promise? The presence of this question in the hearts of men puts deep emphasis on my reason for opening this book with the words: GOD HAS THE MATTER IN HAND.

The Church given to us by Jesus Christ and nourished and protected by Him for the nineteen hundred and sixty years that preceeded the Council, has not vanished from the earth. In fact, the Documents which declare the findings of the Council give rock-bottom assurance of the stability of that Church. The turmoil which has followed, largely from misinterpretation of those Documents, is evidence, often repeated in the history of the Church, that God absolutely refuses to *compel* obedience to His will. Instead, He brings about the results He chooses by His all wise management of the doings of men, be they good or be they evil.

The year 1974 gives much evidence of an approaching climax in this great mystery of God's power to bring good out of evil. What will happen next we do not know. I submit the pages that follow, as I have said, with the conviction that there are very many millions who will rejoice to be assured that the Deposit of Faith given us by Christ and guaranteed by Him in the custody of our Holy Father Pope Paul VI will not be overcome by the Gates Of Hell!

THE THEME OF MY PRESENT OUTLOOK ON THE WORLD STARTS WITH A POEM

GOD HAS THE MATTER IN HAND

There was peace and love in the Trinity
When Creation was planned.
It seemed sad that things should become perverse
But anyway, God took the matter in hand.

Man was made quite able to love
And able to understand.
That meant he could choose what he would love
That's why God took the matter in hand.

God gave him a wife and made him the boss
Of everything in the land.
He chose for himself and defied God's law
But God kept the matter in hand.

Everything went from bad to worse
Until the whole world was manned
By nothing but sinners who still could love
Because God kept the matter in hand.

So God chose Abram out of the East
Because God knew he would stand
When put to the test to offer his son
For he knew God had the matter in hand.

The son of this son, Jacob by name,
Fathered a sizable band –
"God's Chosen People" a stiff necked race
But God kept the matter in hand.

Through hundreds of years they chafed at God's ties
Down to a single strand
But God nursed them along through every breach
For He still had the matter in hand.

No man could know or even guess God's solution
God's solution so utterly grand
That God would Himself come into the world
And take over the matter in hand.

But that's what He did as a tiny Child
So it's called the "Holy Land".
In no other way could all sin be cured
And God have the matter in hand.

If all had been well, such proof of God's love
Would very soon have fanned
A flame of good will in all who saw
That God had the matter in hand.

But sad to relate, the poor little Tot
Had to flee to a foreign land
Or Herod would kill Him along with His mates,
Had not God had the matter in hand.

He proved He was God in dozens of ways
Even devils obeyed His command
But only a few were made to believe
It was God had the matter in hand.

He did all He could to win their love
But at last He had to brand
Their hate for the evil that it was
Then God took the matter in hand.

They hounded Him down to the tree of the Cross
Opened His Heart with a lance — and
Left His Mother alone to know
'Twas God had the matter in hand.

He'd promised to rise so they sealed up His tomb
In response to the High Priest's demand.
It's time, they said, to stop this claim
That God has the matter in hand.

But rise He did and commissioned His Twelve
To tell it in every land.
They did it so well that the number grew
Proving God had the matter in hand.

The Devil once more went into the fray
With imps out-counting sea sand.
We'll see, said he, when I get through
If God keeps the matter in hand.

It's been that way to this very day.
In fact, God had it planned;
You go it alone or else rejoice
That God keeps the matter in hand.

God sends His Angels with mighty power
To spread out over the land
And keep those safe from Satan's raids
Who choose God for the matter in hand.

CHAPTER I

YOU ARE INVITED

The world is fast approaching an age of atheism. Its essential characteristic is the utter blank in the minds of its adherents regarding what believers consider the *only* thing that counts. We are here for one purpose overwhelmingly obvious to one who admits the super-reality of the supernatural. 'We are here by chance' — is the only alternative available to the mind of one who refuses to see that the supernatural *is* obvious. It is a case of infinity versus a little less than zero. So it deserves *everything* that we who see can give.

It is my purpose to amplify the answer to the question: "HOW COME — MY FAITH? " These will not be just the words of believers to atheists. They will be the words of one believer who hopes for and loves the infinite goal, to all his fellows; to those nearer the goal than he, for their support; to those who declare themselves at the zero point, for their attention; and for those legions in between, to help them avoid contamination, even the slightest, by the blatant shouting of materialism. It dins in our ears with increasing clamor as the hidden truths of matter are studied by those in all categories of belief and unbelief.

You are invited, then, to share with me some thoughts about the business of our relationship to God; and that surely is everybody's business because, thank God, a denial of God does not deprive Him of being the most important reality in the life of the one who denies Him.

Furthermore, the words of St. Paul are precisely true today in spite of the oblivion cast upon them by "won't believers" — "It is recorded in men's hearts, their consciences bearing them witness." (Rom. 2:15). In other words, the recognition of the necessity of a Creator is a part of man's very nature. Thinking men with souls and free will are linked to God as no other creatures are, even though some have nearly made themselves believe the contrary.

All this will interest the most devout daily communicant among Catholics as well as those who come to church only on Christmas and Easter. It will also appeal to you who have no intention of entering a church at all unless you can be comfortably carried up the aisle by six men dressed in black.

I am calling good Catholics and Catholics not-so-good as well as those who do not call themselves Catholics at all. I will not argue or debate with you. I will only tell you what I believe God has made known to men. And I will tell you why I believe the true word comes from God. As to truth which God has made known, there can be no argument. As to our reasons for believing that God made it known — these are also provided by God and will always remain the same. Debate will not make them any more or less cogent.

And be assured of this: if you do not wish to believe, you will find plenty of reasons not to believe. No one can be compelled to believe against his will. Remember the little jingle: "A man convinced against his will holds tight the same opinion still." On the other hand, if you really want to believe, or to strengthen your faith, and will pray with confidence, you may be surprised to find how quickly God will come to your aid with that mysterious free gift of His help which we call "Grace".

And here is something still more important. Please do not be frightened away by any personal reason! There is no one so mean that he is not invited. There is no one so good that it is useless for him to read. There is no sinner so determined that he cannot be helped. I love sinners — partly because there is such a nice lot to choose from, and partly because Jesus loves them. Anyone whom He loves is good enough for me. True, He hates sin, but He never hates a sinner.

And so, let me voice His invitation to all: "Come to Me all you who labor and are heavy-laden, and I will give you rest." (Matt. 11:18). These words of Our Lord Jesus Christ follow immediately upon His claim to have all the power to do exactly what He may promise to do. "All things have been delivered to Me by My Father and no one knows the Son except the Father, and no one knows the Father except the Son, and he to whom it is the pleasure of the Son to reveal Him."

He is speaking, then, to those who may go to Mass and receive Holy Communion every day. "Come to Me and learn what I have to say to you to make the burdens of this vale of tears more profitable for everlasting life."

He is speaking to all who fulfill all the duties of good Catholic Christians: "I want to tell you how to make that yoke to be sweet, that burden light."

He is speaking to those who are troubled by the fear that the duties and needs of their daily life are hard to reconcile with their Catholic Faith: "I will give you strength for your labors." "No temptation has overtaken you but such as belongs to human nature, and God is faithful, who will not permit you to be tempted beyond your powers; on the contrary, He will with temptation provide also the escape, so that you will be able to bear it." (I Cor. 10:13). "Come and learn of Me."

For those who may be lukewarm Catholics He has a special word. He wants to tell you just a little of what He has done for you. Christ, if truly known, simply does not admit of half-hearted service.

To those who have had the Faith and have lost it, or

perhaps have even thrown it away, Christ is whispering to your hearts: "Come and hear a little more of my message. It may give you new Hope. Do not ever despair of gaining back that priceless treasure which perhaps you failed to value when you had it. Do not be afraid! "

To those who have never had the Faith, but have sometimes wondered ... You also are heavy-laden. He says: "Ask and it shall be given to you; seek and you shall find; knock and it shall be opened to you." (Matt. 7:7). "Come and learn of Me."

To those to whom the thought of Faith has never come, He who is the True Light which enlightens every man, has come into the world. He is speaking to you now. He will say much to you in the words that follow. Remember, He said: "He who hears you hears Me, and he who hears Me, hears Him who sent Me." (Luke 10:16)

Then, there are so many who assume that all sophisticated people know that science has superseded religion. You may get a hint from Him who is the Way, the Truth and the Life. He is the Author of all science and the Creator of all the things that science knows. He will remind you that in very recent years He has condescended to permit men of science to have an amazing glimpse into what we call His microcosm and His macrocosm. That glimpse has been extremely sobering to some who have held that sense-knowledge and reason alone can furnish the key to all things needful to man.

And there are those dear people who do not yet want to believe. You will not find any words here that need disturb you. The Faith that Christ asks for is the acceptance of Himself as God. It carries with it a complete abandonment of any hostility. It gives a sense of His immense love for every individual soul. His is a love that makes Him willing to offer Himself for one, even one who has made himself hostile to Christ through sin. This Faith cannot take root in a soul until that soul will take Him at His word and allow itself to enter into union with

Him as the moving principle of its will. That is what
Christ meant when He said: "Whosoever believes abides in
Me and I in him."

No one who is pugnatious about the obstacles to belief
is so disposed that he can expect to receive the Grace to
believe. I do not say this to intimate that there are no
obstacles to Faith. There are plenty of them. How well I
know them! There are obstacles now; there were obstacles when Christ began to preach; there will be
obstacles until the end of time. Only one of them, however, is insurmountable. That is the will *not* to believe.
That is the "unforgivable sin" against the Holy Spirit, a
turning away from the known truth about God. When
one has the will not to believe, God will always allow him
to find ways to refuse belief.

God did this when St. Paul, with the vision of the
risen Christ burning in his soul, pleaded with the Jewish
doctors of the law to take the scales from their eyes and
see the truth. They were blinded by a worldly pride and
lust for power. Just so, men today are blinded by the lure
of a way of life that does not square with God's commands concerning their behavior, or by their pride in the
opinions they have held which they might have to admit
were wrong.

And so it will always be. When once a man says to
himself: "If it is true, I should try to believe," then He
has received the first Grace. And when he says: "I believe, Lord, help Thou my unbelief! " then, and only
then, has he begun to find the means of supernatural
Faith.

The Church is Christ's Mystical Body. It is, and ever
will be, the image and the prolongation of Christ's life on
this earth. In His Name it offers the same inducement to
believe Him, the same motives of credibility and the same
ineffable benefits for belief. Ordering all things sweetly as
He did, she is still subject to the same attacks that He
was.

It is not for the appalling faults of her human children that the Church is usually attacked, but rather for the very reasons that Christ was attacked; namely, for her insistence on the primacy of the spiritual; for her insistence that the body is subordinate to the soul; for her insistence that the divine truth and divine law are absolute and are infallibly made known to men.

I want you to see what infinite love has caused Christ to come to us and to remain with us in His Church. I will show you why I believe that Christ is God. And when I do, you may, like me, be utterly amazed to learn that God went to such unspeakable lengths to do so much for such ungrateful souls.

How can it be that those who do not wish to believe, do not find an incentive to believe when they hear the words of everlasting Truth? I will tell you why! It is because divine truth is primarily revealed truth. It is more certain than any other truth knowable to man because its stark reality comes from the Creator of reality, the Center and Author of all being. Yet revealed truth is supernatural, that is, beyond the natural capacity of man's knowledge. To believe revealed truth with divine certainty requires an act which is supernatural Faith. Man cannot perform a supernatural act without the free gift of God's help which, as I have said, we call "Grace".

True, every man receives the offer of this gift of Grace. It is the still, small voice within us which prompts us at certain times to heed the words which come to us from God. But God in His wisdom made man free to resist the offer of Grace. And when Grace is resisted, it is withdrawn and so, strange as it may seem, it then becomes impossible for a man to give the assent of divine faith to the most absolutely certain of all truth. He will always be able to find reasons why he does not choose to believe. That is another of the rather terrifying things about Grace.

When one considers the rewards offered by God for

Faith, it does seem almost impossible to understand why anyone should not wish to believe. But this again is one of the mysteries of Grace. It explains why every new convert is so astonished that it took him so long to find his way, and why he is so distressed to find that his influence has little effect upon his friends who have not yet found the way. It lends weight to the belief that the Angels, who see God's gifts to men in their reality, stand in utter amazement when they observe the choices made by men.

But why should that be? Is not God cruel to make a thing of such great importance so hard to find? No, it is not so hard to find. But it is resisted because the act of supernatural faith involves an obligation of utter submission to, and adoration of, the Creator by the creature. It involves a bending of that proud free will to prostrate at God's feet and say with the meaning of true reality: "Thy will, not mine, be done." It involves the admission that the Creator has the right to say to the creature: "Thou shalt adore the Lord thy God and Him only shalt thou serve." It involves a way of life which, from the outside, looks hard, though again by the mystery of grace, from the inside, can be easy.

He who stands aside and cries: "Non serviam! " "I will not serve! " can seldom hear those consoling words of Christ: "Come to me, all you who labor and are heavy-laden, and I will give you rest. Take My yoke upon you and learn of Me, for I am gentle and humble of heart; and you shall find rest for your souls. For My yoke is easy and My burden light."

But if one wishes to believe, the very reverse is true. The acceptance of God's gift of grace is always and infallibly accompanied by other graces so that one can go on and on until he reaches the goal of true supernatural Faith which Christ referred to when He said: "I ask for those who believe in Me, that as Thou Father, art in Me, and I in Thee, they also may be one in Us, that Thou lovest them as Thou lovest Me." (John 17:23)

YOU ARE INVITED, then, to come with me in this quest for truth. It will be a treasure-hunt worth *all* your time!

Study Questions:

1. Comment on the essential characteristic of *Atheism*.
2. Name and comment on the different classes of people to whom the question: HOW COME — MY FAITH? is addressed.
3. Why is there no occasion for argument or debate with reference to questions of Faith?
4. What is the admonition to grave sinners regarding the subject of this book?
5. What is Christ's word to: daily Communicants, practicing Catholics, troubled Catholics, lukewarm Catholics, fallen-away Catholics, inquirers, sophisticated science students?
6. Comment on the status of those who resist the consideration of the evidence for Faith.
7. Name and comment on what is called "The Unforgivable Sin."
8. Comment on the statement: "The Church is Christ's Mystical Body," and compare it with Christ's own appeal.
9. Why do many refuse "The Words of Everlasting Truth?"
10. Answer the question: "Is not God cruel to make a thing of such great importance so hard to find?"

CHAPTER II
WHY CATHOLICS?

In our quest for Truth we must first learn to confide in Divine Providence. However secret God may at times be, know that He hears every plea and rewards every response to His Grace. Our success in seeking Truth is proportionate to our response to the encouragement God gives us.

The supernatural confidence stemming from this encouragement of Grace reminds me of an experience of its natural counterpart. It always gives me a chuckle, remembering my fishing days before the death of my wife. She and I were fishing together for steelhead. It was·one of those days that go down in memory to make fishing, especially steelhead fishing, something to be hoped for in heaven. I was sitting in the stern of the boat getting the outboard motor ready to "go places" while my wife, standing at the bow, was taking a few casts where the fish were already showing signs of action. A couple of men in an outboard motor skiff were going past us out in the current of the pool. As they went by, one of them, watching my wife casting, shouted over the roar of his outboard motor: "The old gal lays out a pretty good line, doesn't she?" And with that, the "old gal", then only in her thirties, picked up the line off the water and laid it out as beautifully as any woman fly-caster I have ever seen. That was the beginning of the best day we ever had on that river. And so I invite you to make confidence in

God's help an assurance that ours is going to be a successful search after Truth.

It is said that when lovers disagree, they should carefully write down their differences, put them away for a few days, and then burn them. Every priest worthy of the name is a lover of souls. He loves them with his whole heart and soul. Why? Because he *believes* that Jesus Christ is their Creator and Sovereign God. He believes that Jesus loves these souls and wishes him to work for them.

When I finished my studies in Sacred Theology, this burning love for souls made me anxious; there were so many who did not wish to share that love with me by doing the will of Christ. I did some writing to show how this disagreement was injuring both of us because it deprived us of that union in Christ which would be so precious to us.

Then God's Providence put me to teaching in a seminary for many years and I had no time to write. When the opportunity finally came again and I dug out my old writing, I found that what I had written was in a tone that might seem controversial and argumentative. I realized then that I myself had never been moved toward the Faith by argument. It had come to me by simple explanation and still more by the example of those living it, and as I know now, perhaps most of all by the prayer of others in my behalf. And so I decided to follow the warning and burn my first attempt. I resolved to tell you why I love you, instead of trying to make you love me first. Now the reason why I love you can best be answered by telling you *what* I believe, *why* I believe, and *when* one can believe.

We all believe our ordinary store of human knowledge on the authority of someone else who had the time and skill to learn certain items of truth and report them to us with evidence for believing that he observed correctly and reports truthfully. Our faith or belief, based on confidence in the knowledge and truthfulness of another human being, is called "human faith". Human faith may sometimes be deceived but it is usually adequate for all our worldly needs.

But when we wish to know the truth about our relationship to God, we find that human faith is inadequate for two reasons. First: many of the important truths about God are beyond the capacity of human reason to comprehend, even though they are not contrary to reason. Second: purely human evidence about God is so full of conflict and contradiction that human faith alone is destroyed. So the only kind of faith to give conviction about our relationship to God is faith based on confidence that God Himself gave us a revelation about Himself and coupled it with sufficient evidence that we may believe it on the authority of God-Revealing. This we call "divine faith".

We may illustrate the difference between human faith and divine faith by considering an ordinary road map. Mark with a colored pencil all the roads you have actually traveled in your life. Then note that many of the roads you have not traveled recently are changed. And yet you believe that the map is substantially correct. You trust the truth and skill of those who made the map.

And so it is with nearly all our store of human knowledge. We find no difficulty in believing it on the authority of others. But when we begin to look into the truths of religion, we find that the maps which are presented to us are not all alike. Sometimes we are told that these maps all lead to the same destination and it really does not make any difference which route we take. But when we examine the maps we find that some state as true facts what others flatly deny.

Furthermore, these opposite statements of belief are not about unimportant differences of route but often they are about things which mark the difference between success in our journey towards Truth, and complete disaster. For example, one map shows that Jesus Christ is True God and True Man, who voluntarily laid down His life to obtain our eternal salvation. Another map shows that He was a very good man who lost His life because He preached too rashly about an unpopular philosophy of life.

For a person to test the truth of these contradictions one-by-one would be practically impossible because one lifetime would be far too short. Many of the most important religious truths are beyond the power of human reason to prove. They only have value if we know they have been revealed by God.

We must, then, return to the only other open road to find out if one of these non-agreeing road-maps to heaven has all the religious truth we need and no errors.

At this point Satan has contrived a roadblock which has led many astray. Infallible certainty, he says, is beyond the power of human reason, alone. Exactly! but human reason is not alone; it is informed by revelation from an infinitely perfect God. Such a revelation with even the smallest error is simply a contradiction in terms. And the same is true if such a God put forth a revelation to tell man the means of salvation and did not make it possible for man to know that revelation without any error.

But the examination of religious truths one-by-one is ruled out because of lack of time. How can one possibly examine all the hundreds of different institutions teaching religious doctrine? How does one even begin? That question would be practically impossible to answer except that there is one institution with several obvious reasons for examining its credentials first.

The Roman Catholic Church has taught the same body of doctrine longer than any other institution in the world. It is the only church with continuous existence since the death of Jesus of Nazareth, its Founder. But far more important than all the rest, it is the only institution in

OF MT. TABOR

the world which claims infallible protection by God from teaching error. If this claim can be verified, our search for truth has found an open road and everything else falls into line. It is certainly worth a try!

But, you may ask: "If it is as obvious as that, why is the whole world not Catholic? Why, on the contrary, are there so many who hate the Catholic Church? " There are three principal reasons which God has allowed to stand in the way of our immediate acceptance of the doctrine presented for our belief by the Catholic Church.

What God commanded the Church to teach is called by Saint Paul "The Deposit Of Faith". It was given by Jesus Christ to the Apostles chosen by Him for His first Teaching Authority. He promised them and their successors divine protection to guard this Deposit Of Faith and commanded them to "Go and make disciples of all nations . . . teaching them to observe all whatever I have commanded you: and lo, I am with you throughout all time, even until the consummation of the world."

The *what* of this Deposit is not always easy to practice. It forbids some things that fallen human nature wants. Furthermore, it demands a code of moral behavior moved by love of God: to be submissive, obedient, humble, patient, unselfish, temperate, gentle. Every departure from obedience to this Church is attractive to human nature by recommending a relaxation of the moral law or by inviting private interpretation of the manner of worship commanded by God.

Why it is to be believed, rests upon the fact that one Person of the divine Trinity allowed Himself to be born of a Virgin Mother, wife of a poor carpenter among a despised and down-trodden community. His life was humble. His manner was gentle. His doctrine was meek acceptance of the will of God the Father. To all but Jesus, His death appeared to be ignominious defeat. All this is so contrary to the natural inclination of the human will to accept as evidence of divinity that it has been rejected by many all down the centuries *when* it has been offered for belief.

So — having considered some of the obstacles connected with the *what, why,* and *when* of divine faith in the Catholic Church, let us look at a few of the attractions which, in the mind of every well-instructed member of the Church, so far outweigh the obstacles as to make even them attractive.

What Catholics believe is contained in summary form in the Symbol handed down to them by the Apostles of Christ, the "Apostles' Creed". But the essential element which makes Catholics different from other who accept the Apostles' Creed needs some elaboration.

The Apostles' Creed begins: "I believe in God the Father Almighty, Creator of heaven and earth." This much every man *can* know because his God-given reason can enable him to see that the existence of a single thing such as himself or the universe or a grain of sand, which cannot cause itself to be, demands as a cause a Being having the power within its nature to bring into being something out of nothing. This of course, the Atheists refuse to admit. But to a Catholic, every created thing around him speaks of a personal all-wise God as its Author.

The most compelling surge of will-to-believe in my own experience came at the end of another day of steelhead fishing. The light was just fading into dusk and the full moon was just rising over a pool where a small and shallow stream found its way over a long gravel-bar into the head of the pool where I knew there were hundreds of salmon heading for the spawning-grounds, far inland, where they themselves were spawned, there to beget their offspring and then die that their bodies might furnish food for their young.

Every few minutes one of these great salmon would dash up the bar through water only half as deep as his own body, throwing water and even pebbles up on the bank, while he made his way up the bar one hundred yards to the pool above. You might say: "The ways of nature are strange." But I can only say: "How could God tell us more plainly of His guiding hand on all that He has made? "

But let us return to the Apostles Creed which continues: "And in Jesus Christ, His only Son, our Lord, who was conceived by the Holy Spirit, born of the Virgin Mary:" This bit of knowledge is utterly useless to the Catholic unless he has satisfied himself that he knows it with absolute certainty on the authority of God's revelation, because it could not be known with compelling certainty by any human means. But with the certainty of God's revelation, it becomes the center and all-sufficient foundation of all the rest of one's faith.

The next phrase of the Apostles Creed is the only one that all agree could be known with sufficient certainty on the basis of human faith alone: "He suffered under Pontius Pilate, was crucified, died and was buried:" But this is certainly *not* true of the phrases which follow: "He descended into hell, the third day He rose again from the dead, He ascended into heaven, sitteth at the right hand of God the Father Almighty". . .

That True God could die in His Humanity, is no less impossible for man to fabricate out of his own imagination, than that He could revive that dead body by His own power. And as for placing it at the right hand of God's glory — what nonsense that would be were it not confirmed by a supernatural guarantee beyond the possibility of error. Yet *with* such a guarantee, it places the whole human race *and* every individual member of it on a pedestal of dignity equal to that of the angels.

To continue with the Creed: "Thence He shall come to judge the living and the dead." This brief sanction of the entire moral law, couples a responsibility with belief which is a tragic barrier to belief, and practically the only one. This truth which has not yet entered into time, could not even be guessed at without the authority of God-revealing.

"I believe in the Holy Spirit". . . Three Persons in one God is a mystery the "how" of which is quite beyond the reach of man's knowledge even when it is believed on God's authority.

The "what" contained in the next four words of the Creed includes the difference between the belief of Catholics and that of all non-Catholic Christians. The words are: "The Holy Catholic Church."

The invitation of Christ to all men living today hinges upon the true meaning of these four words. They are understood by Catholics as follows:

The Babe of Bethlehem whose Mother and foster father fled with Him to Egypt and then to Nazareth, grew under their human authority in obscurity and poverty until, at about thirty years of age, He emerged as Jesus of Nazareth whose public career began when He was pointed out by the Prophet, John the Baptist, as the Divine Savior of the world.

He continued in the same status of humble simplicity. He extolled poverty, detachment from worldly honor, acceptance of suffering, trials and persecution for the sake of righteousness. *But* His teaching was with the utter confidence of One possessing "all power in heaven and on earth." Gentle: Yes, but with authority beyond all human comprehension. "No man ever spoke like this before" (or since). (John 7:46).

But another part of His life means the most to us in the twentieth century. He chose twelve men whom He designated as the first ministers of His Church, who, with their successors, would be His witnesses for all time, bringing the Good News of His doctrine to every man to be born into the world.

As the end of His life drew near, He appointed Simon Peter as the head of these first Bishops of His Church. He taught them how God wishes to be worshipped from that hour until the end of time. But — more important than all else — He promised them that He would send His Holy Spirit who would dwell within them and bring to their minds all that He had commanded them to teach, and would protect them for all time against teaching error. He promised, too, that He Himself would also dwell with them "until the consummation of the world."

His first priests set about their work with fortitude and a success only possible with divine aid — teaching all things He had commanded them. And this they have done ever since in spite of the most determined persecution the world has ever seen. It made martyrs of most of the Popes for the first three hundred years.

And here is something equally important! Between twenty and seventy years after they were endowed by Christ with this precious gift of infallible Teaching Authority, they and their immediate assistants wrote, to help them in their work, the letters and Gospels which now constitute the New Testament of the Bible.

The writers of these documents were "inspired" by God. That is, they wrote what God intended them to say. But the documents themselves have no guarantee of infallibility. They are only the tools of Christ's Teaching Authority.

It is to *men* and those taught by them that Christ gives His guarantee. These men have defended the Bible through the centuries against many, not divinely appointed, who have contradicted their interpretation of its meaning. Unauthorized private interpretation of the meaning of the Bible has led many into heresy and schism. Their action is no more legitimate than it would be for me to take the Anglican Book of Common Prayer and tell their people that it means something different from what they say it means.

So, this is what Catholics believe is meant when they recite the Apostles Creed and say: "I believe in the Holy Catholic Church;" — the same today as it was when it was first commissioned by Christ to teach all men – the infallible source of the answer to every problem of faith and moral conduct.

The final words of the Apostles Creed continue with a catalogue of riches in four items which, if guaranteed by God, are so precious that no treasure on this earth can be compared with any of them. 1. The Communion of Saints – that blessed institution which changes the death of a loved one from black despair into a calm and almost happy interlude. 2. The forgiveness of sins – that gateway to peace which, when really understood, makes life tolerable and hell conquerable. 3. The resurrection of the body, and 4. Life everlasting. What possible earthly joy can be compared with these last two?

This, then, is the important *"what"* that Catholics believe. It gives them peace and utter conviction that their road-map to heaven can be depended upon without fail.

Why do they believe it? For one reason only. Because they believe that Jesus Christ is God whose promises cannot fail! Their reason for *this* belief we will study soon. Here, we can say – *when* one has learned to say with Simon Peter: "We steadfastly believe and know that Thou art the Holy One of God:" – *then* it seems incredible that anyone who really examines the evidence can fail to fall at His feet and adore Him saying: "Lord, I believe, help Thou my unbelief." (Mark 9:23).

Do *you* realize what it means to know that Christ is God? It means an absolutely certain answer to three all-important propositions. 1. God exists. 2. Every word that Christ spoke was God's public revelation to man. 3. There is an infallible means of knowing what God revealed because He promised a Teaching Authority and what God wills cannot fail and God cannot deceive or be deceived. The Catholic Faith needs no other credential than the certainty that Christ is God.

If I could help you to think through all that is implied

in the certain knowledge that Christ is True God — if you could follow that through to its conclusion — ponder it deep in your heart — I would thank Christ for allowing me to be His instrument to help you to learn to know His will, the will of God, and to say on your knees to Him: "Thy will be done!"

Study Questions:

1. Comment on the necessity of confidence in God's help in the quest for *truth*.
2. Comment on the futility of controversy in presenting the *truth* about God.
3. Show why human faith alone is inadequate to explain the *Truth* about God and tell what else is necessary.
4. Illustrate the deficiency of human faith for clinching divine truth by the example of road-maps.
5. Discuss the variation in the "road-maps-to-heaven" and show the impossibility of a purely human solution.
6. Discuss the solution suggested and answer the question: "If it is an obvious as that, why is the whole world not Catholic?" naming the principal obstacles.
7. Explain the essential element which makes Catholics different from others who accept the *Apostles' Creed*, and apply it to the items of the Creed.
8. Discuss the meaning to Catholics of the four words: "The Holy Catholic Church."
9. Discuss the status of the *New Testament* as a source of knowledge of *Divine Truth*.
10. Discuss the one ultimate reason why Catholics accept their *"Road Map to Heaven."*

CHAPTER III
EVIDENCE

I could hardly suppress a chuckle here and there while writing the previous chapter, thinking of the rage which my bland unsupported statements of faith arouse in the minds of those who subscribe wholeheartedly to the credo of atheism. But my road map has a destination. My presentation of the credo of supernatural faith is, as near as I can make it, a sample of the only procedure available to the atheist. He simply shuts the supernatural out of his thinking and assumes that is the end of the argument. He does not attempt to prove his denial because, of course, there is no proof such as we must demand.

And here lies the whole problem of the Christian apologist. The supernatural *is* the true basic reality of *all* that is. All that we experience with our senses or can bring into our sense knowledge, is real only to the degree that it is held in being by the True Reality who is God. He is absolutely unavailable to our senses except as we perceive the necessity of His reality in the universe we live in when we are aided by grace.

And there is the rub! The atheist, by his very creed, closes the access of his soul to grace. In fact, he closes a double door because his creed flatly denies the possession of a soul. So, he has erected a double barricade against grace — wholly supernatural and residing in the soul. This should make it fairly obvious that the Christian apologist has no access in himself to the soul of the atheist. The only access possible is a supernatural one and that seems rather dim since the apologist knows that God will not compel the acceptance of the gift of grace.

The reader may be a little impatient at this point because I am still pursuing the only course open to atheists — declaring prodigious truths without supporting evidence. You may be inclined to remark scornfully with the atheist: "Where did you get all that nonsense? " So I will tell you and perhaps the atheist will listen in.

The Catholic Faith has very much in it that is mere history and sense knowledge but it is a pitiful shame that in the past it has been thought essential to defend it solely on the basis of so-called "scientific" history which records only that which has been available to sense knowledge and does not admit of interpretation beyond that which can be proven as sense knowledge.

Untold harm has been done by admitting the claim that such a proof is necessary or possible. It is not necessary or possible because the entire structure of Catholic Faith rests on one fact that cannot be proved with certainty by *that kind* of historical research — the fact that Jesus of Nazareth is God.

The chief reason that the purely historical approach is not available is that the documents of the New Testament which contain most of the information, are definitely vulnerable to attack as sources of *that kind* of historical data. When this is thoroughly understood, then the evidence which these documents *do* furnish becomes not only infinitely more convincing, but also a *kind* of evidence which is infinitely more useful as a source of the information we seek.

The point is that none of the New Testament Gospels or letters was written with the faintest notion of making historical texts of them in the sense in which that term is usually applied. They were all written precisely for the purpose of giving evidence for the great supernatural drama in which the writers had been actors as well as witnesses.

They felt themselves bound by the command of God: "Go and make disciples of all nations, baptizing them in the name of the Father and of the Son and of the Holy Spirit; teaching them to observe all whatever I have commanded you: and lo, I am with you throughout all time, even until the consummation of the world!" (Matt. 28:19-20). They are testimonial documents written by ardent believers to invite all men to share in the great supernatural treasure of which they have been appointed the custodians.

The nature of the evidence of the authenticity of the New Testament documents is by no means a series of clinching proofs as to what was said and done by Jesus of Nazareth and those with whom He lived. It is a prodigious mosaic involving not only all that has been written including the Old Testament but also all that has been said and done whether recorded or not, by thousands and millions of people all down the centuries to the present day.

The "Church-Believing" from its very beginning when three thousand people staked their lives on the report given to them by St. Peter, is only a sample of the mosaic which unfolds an invitation to believe that is pregnant with grace.

The rulers of the Jewish people saw in it only the possibility of interference with their worldly prestige and power. They continued, therefore, to behave as they had before the crucifixion of Christ. It was then that they said: "What are we about? for this man is working many miracles. If we let him go on like this, everybody will believe in Him and the Romans will come and take away both our place and our nation." (John 11:47). Thus they closed the door to grace.

All was changed, however, after the first Pentecost.

Fervor saturated the minds of those who had been in that upper room and heard and saw what took place there. They gave evidence that made headway in spite of every frantic move to exterminate them. And this continued with ever-growing force and ever-growing numbers until the record of it was put down in writing in the four Gospels and the Epistles of Saint Paul.

These Gospels and Epistles were not written as mere reports of what had taken place in the past. They were put in writing as a continuation of the impassioned plea of the preachers who had given their all to bring Christ to souls. They simply carried on the confessional preaching which, in the face of persecution and strife and hardship, had won unimaginable success for the very reason that its evidence was so obviously supported by supernatural aid.

The persecution stemmed from those who closed their minds to grace. The success came from those who opened their minds and wills to what they heard and saw and thus made themselves eligible for grace.

The fourth chapter of the Acts of the Apostles gives a typical example. It was written by Saint Luke after it had been reported for many years by all the pleaders for Christ. Most of those who had knowledge of it were still alive to verify its truth.

The Apostles Peter and John had been thrown into prison for healing a cripple in the presence of a large crowd at the gates of the Temple. Then Saint Luke continues the story:

"On the following day their princes, ancients and scribes assembled at Jerusalem . . . and placing them in the midst they inquired. 'By whose power or in whose name have you done this? '

Then Peter, filled with the Holy Spirit said to them: 'Princes of the people and ancients, if we are under examination today regarding a benefit to an infirm man — by what means he has been cured — let it be known to you all, and to all the people of Israel, that by the *name* of Jesus Christ the Nazarene,

whom you crucified, whom God raised from the dead, by Him
this man stands in your presence, well.' . . . .
Now . . . looking at the man who had been cured standing
with them, they had no contradiction to offer. But ordering
them to retire from the Council they conferred among themselves, saying, 'What shall we do with these men? For that a
notable miracle has been done through them is manifest to all
the inhabitants of Jerusalem, and we cannot deny it. But that
it may spread no further among the people, let us warn them
with threats to speak no more to any man in this name.' Then,
having recalled them, they forbade them to speak or teach at
all in the *name* of Jesus. Peter and John, however, said to
them in reply, 'Judge whether it is right in God's sight to
listen to you rather than to God. For we cannot do otherwise
than tell what we have seen and heard.' " (cf. Acts 4:1-20).

The absurdity of flat denial by today's atheist of all
this supernatural inference, becomes apparent if we
examine the only two "outs" available to them. First,
they may say that the faith of these first five thousand
believers or the millions that have followed them was won
by a clever trickery of Jesus and His followers. Second,
they have even affirmed that the writings of the New
Testament were manufactured by the die-hard adherents
of a losing cult long after the true story was forgotten.
The injection of the miraculous was a last-ditch artifice to
save defeat.

There is a faint third alternative. It is sometimes
claimed that all of these men and their constantly increasing followers really brought themselves to believe what
never really happened. It is suggested that their ardent
wish that it had been true induced some kind of mass-hallucination extending over a whole lifetime and a whole
generation of victims and through them reaching to the
present day.

The first conjecture, that of treacherous deceit, is not
called such by its inventors. They merely state that Jesus,
a well-intentioned peasant, succeeded in gaining quite a
following until His rash opposition to the leaders of the
Jews brought about His crucifixion. But by that time His

followers were so far inebriated by His teaching that they stole His Body from the tomb and had amazing success as a result of claiming His Resurrection from the dead. But none of this was accompanied by any supernatural occurrences either physical or spiritual. And the clinching proof of it all is that such occurrences are impossible. It is assumed by the atheists. as indeed it must be assumed, that no further proof is needed.

One could go on from here, page after page, reciting the inadequacy of the claim of "impossibility" as a proof of the non-occurence of the "apparent" supernatural accompaniment of much of the words and actions of Jesus throughout the three years of His public life. The reader might amuse himself by imagining an explanation for each of the tremendous variety of apparent miracles performed. They usually took place in the presence of a crowd and each required the connivance of a number of people all of whom must be trusted to carry out the deception with no apparent benefit to themselves.

The preposterous inadequacy, however, of the whole theory of deception is emphasized in the consideration of the one great event which could have occurred without any supernatural concomitant, the crucifixion of Jesus himself. What possible motive can be suggested to explain His bull-headed tenacity in sticking to the one basic claim for which He was subjected to a death of torture? Why did He persistently hold on to the claim that made the Jews shout before Pontius Pilate: "We have our own law, and by our law He ought to die, for pretending to be the Son of God." (John 19:7 Knox). When all is said and done, that claim was the one reason for His crucifixion and it is necessary to claim that He knew it was a lie!

But still more difficult to explain without supernatural backing is the loyalty and indomitable courage of His Apostles after His death and disappearance from the tomb. The crucifixion obviously brought complete collapse to all their expectations. They were at first utterly incredulous of the reports that Jesus had risen from His grave. They went back to their fishing boats and remained in obscurity for several weeks.

Later, they assembled in the Cenacle at Jerusalem and there was some kind of disturbance that brought several thousand people into their vicinity. Then they came out so utterly changed in their whole being that they were able to convince a multitude that had no previous notion of believing. And, more impossible still, Peter and John were emboldened to defy the supreme court of Jewish law, the officers of the Sanhedrin. That same loyalty and dedication continued without a break, in the face of continued bitter persecution and martyrdom. The same is true, with every conceivable variation, of the entire history of the Church up to the present day.

And so the apparent impossibility of explaining all this on a natural basis has led to the second alternative for denial of the reality of the supernatural — the assertion that it was invented when the documents of the New Testament were put in writing. This had perhaps a vestige of plausibility when it was asserted that none of the New Testament as we have it now, came into being until the third or fourth century. Biblical research, however, has demolished that theory. All now agree that the writings were made during the first century and represented the teaching that had prevailed in the Church from the beginning.

The worth of this theory, however, can perhaps be best appraised by asking the question, "If the amazing growth of the Church prior to the assembling of the books of the New Testament had been accomplished without the backing of supernatural aid — without the resurrection of Christ — without His ascension into heaven — without the miracle of Pentecost — why in the world was it thought necessary to deceitfully insert it when there were many thousands who had been living throughout the life of the Infant Church who would know that it was false? "

The third possibility; that of considering mass-hallucination as the source of the lasting deception of the reality of the supernatural, becomes so entangled in the variety and extent of the phenomena that it practically falls of its own weight.

The inevitable fact of the reality of the supernatural thus seems to stand in the way opposing the will of the atheist, the materialist and the agnostic. They, however, appear to be unaware that there is cause for bafflement or even of the fact that bafflement exists. They are very much in the situation of Balaam whose transportation on an ass was halted when the ass became aware of an Angel of the Lord in her path and refused to carry Balaam any further. And, just as Balaam had no recourse but to fall to beating the unfortunate ass, so the atheist has no recourse but to shout invective against such general terms as soul, faith, religion and God.

Here are a few samples of the way it is expressed:

Of course, all religious dogmas are at war with objectivity and logic.

Any sort of faith is an outrage to intelligence. The future belongs to statistical probability.

Seeing nothing of value, and much of harm in your organization, I am happy to see you riding to your well-deserved oblivion.

You are a pathetic spectacle of the local religious brain-washing process.

Your very concept of a soul is completely ridiculous.

You have far too much on the ball to get mesmerized by any man-made religion that was built on the multi-god monstrosity the Greeks imagined and the Romans re-did with a slightly different decor.

We are a happy crew. Far from having to worry about arousing the ire of certain supernatural agencies, we have a far more difficult assignment of keeping our stock of knowledge growing. But we are happy to leave the simple creeds and the catechisms to the simple minds and the dupes. I advise you to join our small crew. It is far more fun than repeating endless prayers to postulated supernatural agencies who stubbornly refuse to give any statistically valid evidence of their existence.

There are no worse sadists than those who would force a child upon any female who does not want it. They are the worst of criminals.

People will not long tolerate the psychological pressures against contraception. They will simply remake their gods and their moralities in adjustment with their material world. Since there never was a god that man himself did not create, that will be no great task. Gods and moral codes are a dime a dozen. Thousands have existed and more will emerge. I am appalled at the egotism of each little batch of believers that assumes that its god is eternal and timeless.

As for the chances that the Roman Church is the mouthpiece of divine wisdom, they are so remote and incredible that I would have to abandon every grain of wisdom and experience *even* to consider the statistics of its probability!

And so it goes – on and on. Balaam's ass still refuses to move in the face of the incontrovertible proof of the reality of the supernatural while Balaam goes on beating the poor creature with invective. He never touches the point at issue, however, because he "would have to abandon every grain of wisdom and experience even to consider the statistics of its probability."

God finally allowed Balaam to see the Angel in his way but today, as in the day of St. Paul: "If our Gospel is veiled, then the veil thereof is on them that are perishing; for in their case the god of this world hath blinded their incredulous minds, that they should not discern the illumination of the Gospel of the glory of Christ, who is the image of God." (II Cor. 4:3-4).

And all the while the amazing story presents itself to all who will "consider the statistics of its probability." But it is closed to those who refuse. There is, of course, even in the present time, incontrovertible evidence of miracles available to those whose credo does not prevent them from examining the evidence. But the prodigious mosaic furnished by God and His Church does not lend itself to argument or debate. It is futile to attempt an item-by-item examination of the evidence of authenticity of the writings that tell the story of the Church and its people down the centuries.

Father Avery Dulles, S.J., sums up the only attitude for appraising the authenticity of Scripture which is consistent with the circumstances under which it came about.

As to the Resurrection of Christ, he says: "All the criteria which point to authentic revelation are magnificently verified." (*Apologetics & Biblical Christ*, p. 58). All report the same event integrally; all show that it was utterly unexpected; all show themselves totally transformed by the experience.

And Father Dulles concludes: "A religion so lofty in content, so novel, so unanimous, so self assured, so effortless, so joyful, so fruitful in good works, so durable in adversity, such a religion has all the marks of a divine revelation." (ibid p. 40)

All this brings it about that: "Men earnestly seeking communion with God can find in the Bible a solid warrant for belief." (ibid p. 59).

Study Questions:

1. Explain the status of the atheist with respect to the approach of the Christian apologist.

2. Discuss the inadequacy of "scientific history" to furnish proof of the truth of divine revelation.

3. Compare the response of the Jewish rulers to the events recorded in the Gospels with that of the disciples who witnessed the first Pentecost.

4. Explain the motive of the writers of the Gospels and Epistles of the New Testament.

5. Describe the two "outs" used by the atheist for denial of the supernatural evidence found in the writings of the New Testament.

6. Discuss the inadequacy of these "outs".

7. How is the plight of Balaam to be compared to that of the denier of the supernatural?

8. Quote samples of the atheist's invective against religion and comment on it.

9. Give the gist of St. Paul's comment on the veil over the Gospel message.

10. Comment on Father Avery Dulles' appraisal of the authenticity of Scripture.

CHAPTER IV

WHY PROTESTANTS?

In North America in the twentieth century the separation and, at times, opposition that exists between the Catholic Church and other Christian Churches stems from accepted tradition rather than from examination and rejection. G. K. Chesterton's comment as to Christianity in general was: "Christianity has not been tried and found wanting — it just hasn't been tried." In these days the same idea applies to the traditional separation between the Catholic Church and most of the human beings who are not her members. It is not that they have examined the teaching of the Catholic Church and found it false; it is just that it has never crossed their minds that there is any reason why they should examine it.

They have been brought up from infancy in an atmosphere that ranges all the way from pure atheism to profession of belief in all that has been revealed by Christ. Those of the former category stop short of examining any religion because they have always taken it for granted that it is superstitious nonsense. The latter take for granted the traditional cliches about the betrayal of the promises of Christ by the corrupt Catholic clergy when they introduced "Mary Worship" and all the fear-engendering dogmas of "Popery".

The net result is that there is an abysmal blank in the minds of most of the non-Catholics in North America as to any reason why the Catholic Church presents an incentive for their attention in preference to the milieu in which they now live.

The fact is that the present situation of the Catholic Church in North America is characteristic of her history from the time that Christ commanded His first Bishops to go out and teach the world. During the past four hundred years, most of the Christian groups which originally separated from the Catholic Church in the sixteenth century are called or call themselves "Protestants".

Nowadays, however, there is little advertence to the fact that the name specifies a protest against the teachings of the Catholic Church. Protestants simply share with all other non-Catholics the notion that their beliefs have emancipated them from an outworn cult that clings to ancient superstitions which have been discarded by modern scientific knowledge. Very few of them know anything about the nature of these so-called "ancient superstitions".

The term 'Protestant', then, is new in the past four hundred years but the behavior of protestantism has repeated itself many times in the past. It starts from within the Church and usually results from a rebellion against the absolute bed-rock necessity with which Christ guaranteed the perpetuity of His Church.

This guarantee secures the integrity of all that has been revealed by God to man and causes it to mesh with man's ever-changing world environment. It is basically 'managed' by the Holy Spirit. But its adjustment to the Church and to the world as a going-concern is exercised through the Magisterium or Teaching Authority headed by the Holy Father, the Pope of Rome.

This divine infallible protection of the revealed will of God as to the faith, the worship, and the moral behavior of the members of His Church is the one thing without which it could not possibly endure, as Christ has promised, until the end of time. It is the one indispensable asset of the Church and yet it is perhaps the greatest stumbling-block to the Protestant. And here again, the principal reason that it is despised is that it is misunderstood.

The doctrine of Infallibility, as it is called, would very rightly be despised by all men if it claimed what the scoffer usually believes it to mean; namely, that God has promised to give the Pope such infinite wisdom that he can never make a mistake or do any wrong.

Actually, the doctrine of Infallibility does not claim for the Pope any power different from that given to other men. What is precisely true is that the doctrine of Infallibility claims action by God rather than action by any man. It simply professes a trust in the promises made by Christ that the Revelation brought by Him from God the Father in heaven would be available to all men of all time without distortion or diminution or addition.

Christ did not promise that each believing Christian would be individually made aware of this Revelation. He promised that the Teaching Authority chosen by Him and commanded by Him to go into the world and be available to all men, would teach this Revelation under the immediate guardianship of His Holy Spirit. It is really the ever-present Spirit of Christ who exercises Infallibility rather than the Pope and Bishops acting in their official capacity.

It is true, they are obliged in conscience to use the utmost of their natural powers, as St. Paul admonished St. Timothy, to "Guard the Deposit of Faith! Avoid profane and fruitless discussions and disputations of 'knowledge' falsely so styled, which some have professed and have erred in faith." (I Tim. 6:29).

The Holy Father and His Bishops are assured that, if they faithfully follow this advice of St. Paul and have as their aim the strengthening and clarifying of Revelation, they will be helped by the Holy Spirit to a right declaration of that Revelation.

And only here is where the promise of infallibility becomes operative. It simply means that, if the Holy Father, or the Bishops of the world with the approval of the Holy Father, as a result of malice, self-will, ignorance, carelessness, fear or all else, should be prepared to declare to the world as revealed by God any item of faith or any law of human behavior which contains any error whatever, their decision would be prevented by God from being declared.

It may be that there have been Popes or Bishops in the past against whom this sort of action has been necessary. But the Popes and most of the Bishops of the present century have shown themselves to be of very different character and have cherished the guidance of the Holy Spirit. Nevertheless, with or without their good will, we have God's promise that their decisions can be depended upon with certainty. And *that* is the doctrine of Infallibility. It is God's action and not man's magic.

When one considers the hundreds of Christian sects and realizes that they all stem from some form of denial of God's promise of infallible protection, God's reason for making that promise seems very clear to the believer.

It is a matter of history, however, that the constant cooperation of the Holy Spirit goes far beyond the legalistic application of the doctrine of Infallibility. It gives the believer a guarantee that Christ's Church, with His Vicar at its head, will be the source of salvation until the end of time. But it is in this area that protestantism of every kind has its beginning. Disobedience and disallegiance of individuals or groups of individuals to the Holy Father and the constant teaching of the Church, have been and are now the ever-present source of protestantism. It boils up after every General Council and is rampant today to the heart-break of the Holy Father.

Once the promise of Christ is despised in any detail, it blossoms into departures in every direction and so division is multiplied. And that is the answer to the question: Why are Protestants?

The natural sequel to this separation is oblivion as to the grounds for faith and forgetfulness as to its true nature. Every division of Protestantism presents a different set of objections but denial of Infallibility must be common to all. And, strange as it may seem, this is coupled with coldness toward the Blessed Virgin Mary, Mother of God, except in the separated Churches of the East.

The pity of this coldness is emphasized in the text from the Book of Proverbs which is a eulogy of the supernatural gift of Wisdom and is applied to Our Lady in much of the liturgy in her honor. Here is the way it is expressed: *Hear instruction and be wise, and refuse it not. Blessed is the man that heareth me . . . He that shall find me, shall find life, and drinks deep of the Lord's favor, he who fails shall hurt his own soul; to be my enemy is to be in love with death.* (Prov. 8:33-36).

Catholics do not attribute any supernatural powers directly to the Blessed Virgin. It grieves them tremendously that their love for her and their respect for the prerogatives with which she has been endowed by God should be misinterpreted as a superstition and creature-worship by those who have not realized that it is her relationship to God that has made her loved and lovable.

This plea to "hear instruction and be wise" is put on her lips because Christ, on the Cross, gave her to us as our spiritual Mother. It is because of this relationship to all of us that our Holy Mother, the Catholic Church, presents it through the Blessed Virgin to all men.

Christ has made it a special duty of His priests to strive with all their might to overcome the atmosphere of distrust which hinders non-Catholics from learning the truth about the Catholic Church. But these priests can

never succeed unless they are supported by a strong
apostolic spirit on the part of lay Catholics.

There are two chief obstacles to reconciliation with the
Catholic Church. One is the reluctance of Catholic lay
people to recognize their share of this duty of apostolic
zeal; the other is the failure of individual Catholic priests
and lay people to give an example that is consistent with
their faith. When the Catholic Church has to defend itself,
it is not only a sign that someone outside has been
denying the faith, but also that someone inside has been
betraying it.

The removal of these obstacles is the object closest to
my heart. The reason that it is close to my heart is that,
until I was forty-one years old, I belonged to the throng
of those who are separated from the Catholic Church
because of things which they believe that they know, but
which happen to be untrue.

I was definitely anti-Catholic. Most of my antagonism
stemmed from the many shocking things about the Catholic Church, Catholic people and Catholic doctrine
which were so firmly fixed in my mind that one would
almost have to say that I knew them, and yet most of
them were untrue. I say: 'most of them', because obviously there are shocking things that *are* true about the
lives of individual Catholics, individual priests, and even
four or five of the Popes who reigned between the ninth
and the sixteenth centuries, as well as one of the twelve
Apostles chosen by Christ Himself.

I know that "cradle" Catholics often fail to realize
how the behavior of bad Catholics, both present and far
back in history, clinches in the minds of non-Catholics
the conviction that the Catholic Church has betrayed
Christ's command to teach the truth, just as Judas betrayed Christ Himself. These non-Catholics, not having
access to the true doctrine of the Catholic Church, form
their ideas of it from the common misinterpretation of
bad example, coupled with the malicious lies which have

been propagated through the centuries by those who have hated the Church for the same reasons that evil men hated Christ.

The animosity of most anti-Catholics today stems, just as mine did, not altogether from ignorance of the truth, but from being so certain of some things that are *not* true. I was a militant Protestant. I was perfectly certain that my Church had taken over when the Catholic Church had failed at the time commonly called the Reformation.

God, in His mercy and with infinite patience, gradually brought home to me the impossibility of that notion. The reason that it is impossible is, as I have said, that Christ promised that His Church would not fail or teach error. If Christ is God, His promise could not fail. If He is not God, Christianity is nonsense and we, of all men, are the most pitiable. This idea infuriated me because I was so sure that there must be some other answer. That is why I now know quite well that, when badly stated, this idea still infuriates most non-Catholics because they have grown up in the notion that there must be some other answer.

Indeed, there have been dozens of ideas formulated with the intention of giving some other answer which will allow one to avoid the necessity of reaching an unequivocal combat with the problem. Those who see the devastating folly of a denial of the divinity of Christ, try to explain the apparent failure of the Church by attaching the loss of continuity of the Catholic Church to the behavior of individual sinners. They come out with one of two possible solutions: Either they name some denomination which they now call the true Church, saying that it saved the promises of Christ when the hierarchy of the Catholic Church betrayed their trust; or they posit some nebulous invisible church which now gives the individual Christian direct access to the divine Christ in heaven and aids him in whatever body he places himself by common prayer and common worship.

But a far greater number than is imagined by the average church-going non-Catholic, face the issue to the point where they see the necessity of denying at least part of the full Godhood of Jesus of Nazareth. Let us examine this conclusion a little more carefully so as to see why it must be faced, and why, if faced, it is so devastating to the stability of the non-Catholic believer in the divinity of Christ.

I have said that I was infuriated by the notion that explicit belief that Jesus of Nazareth was true-God demands acceptance of the Roman Catholic Church of the twentieth century as the only possible sequel to the examination of the evidence at hand. I can, therefore, readily and with sympathy understand why the same proposition provokes the same emotion in the hearts of the thousands of non-Catholics who, like myself, in response to the question: "Do you believe in the Divinity of Christ? " would have answered: "Yes, certainly I do."

I do not remember exactly how it began to enter my mind that such an admission poses an unanswerable problem to the non-Catholic Christian, but this is the way it began to take shape: There are only two possible ways of knowing that Jesus of Nazareth is God. One way is to accept the New Testament story as authentic in the manner outlined in the previous chapter and observe that He claimed to be God and proved it by acts necessitating the power of God, namely, by notable miracles. The other way is to accept a continuous tradition handed down from one generation to the next by witnesses whose trustworthiness is beyond question.

Now, both of these routes are accessible to every one in the world today. But both are inextricably coupled with the certainty that, in addition to proving that He was God, Jesus said that He was founding a Church upon Saint Peter with the other Apostles as his colleagues.

Christ also promised that this Church and Teaching Authority would act in His Name without fail until the end of time. At another time He promised that He would be with this Teaching Authority personally and in His Holy Spirit, 'until the consummation of the world.' Thus it would be the Holy Spirit who would give them divine and infallible protection against forgetting or leaving out anything that Christ had taught the Apostles, or from adding anything to it, or from changing the substance of it.

Now, to be a Christian and not a Roman Catholic, one must believe that part of the doctrine taught by the Catholic Church is false. Since no other Christian body of doctrine even claims to go back to the Apostles except through the Catholic Church, it follows that the non-Catholic must hold that the promise of Christ has failed. There are only three possible explanations: First, that Christ did not know that evil men would disobey His command; Second, that Christ was unable to prevent evil men from disobeying His command; Third, that the record or tradition that He made the promise and command is false or forged.

Since the record and tradition have come to us only through the successors of the men who received the command and the promise, the third possibility becomes a special instance of the first or second. But that Christ did not know what the future would bring or did not have the power to carry out His promise, contradicts the premise that He is God.

To a Catholic, this is his reason for being a Catholic. To a non-Catholic, it is an aggravating or, as I have called it, an infuriating annoyance which stands in the way of comfortable acceptance of what the Catholic Church calls heresy or schism. Men all down the centuries have wrestled with this unanswerable question. Many, perhaps most, non-Catholics simply put it aside with the comment expressed or implied that "fifty million Protestants can't be wrong." But what an unhappy foundation for the basic principles of one's faith!

For those who do grapple with the question, there is no 'via media'. One either becomes a Catholic or must find some category less than divinity for the Founder of Christianity. Some try to reach a compromise by finding various ways of suggesting that Christ did not mean what the record says He meant. If so, Christ used very direct and simple language to deceive us. That is impossible for God.

Now, to readers who are not Catholics, these words may seem as if I were innocent enough to expect that your reaction would be: "Why! I never thought of that before — but of course it is true, and I will join the Catholic Church immediately." No, I know it is not as simple as it sounds. There are many obstacles in the way, but the only insurmountable one is the will *not* to believe. That is the unforgivable sin against the Holy Spirit which, even though the evidence were coercive, would cause Almighty God to withhold grace without which one cannot make a supernatural act of faith.

No, even with the will to believe, there are obstacles. How well I know them! But I beg you not to set the problem aside simply because it is annoying. In my own experience, as I have said, God in His goodness kept the unanswerable question before me until I saw the truth, but why He was so patient with me I will never know! The means God chose to help me to see the truth was to give me for thirty years a precious Catholic wife, but I am ashamed to admit that it took eighteen of those years for the example of her steadfast faith and saintly behavior, to lead me to learn the truth, first-hand, from a Catholic priest.

Even then, I told the priest that I did not see how I could ever become a Catholic. I admitted, however, that the claim of the Catholic Church to have the infallible truth from God, to have the real Presence of God Himself in the tabernacle and in the Eucharist, to have the true Sacrifice of Calvary continued in the Mass, to have the power of God bestowed upon His priests to forgive sins and to consecrate His Body and Blood; in short, to be the only true Church, with God Himself as its Founder and Head and Life Principle: all this is so prodigious that I would be a fool if I did not learn the doctrine and study the evidence.

The priest was willing to take me under these circumstances and so we grappled with the doctrine for a year and a half until I finally came to see that it all hinged on that fearsome question: Did I believe that Christ is God?

As a last resort, I went to the Pastor of my Church and told him my story about as I have told it to you, and asked him if he could suggest a solution. Again, unexpectedly, his reply gave me tremendous help in a direction other than he had intended. He said: "Our Church teaches all that the Roman Church teaches except what Rome has corrupted or added." In other words, his only foundation of faith rested on the implied claim that the promise of Christ had failed. And what was his authority for this claim? — his own private judgment, based on the Protestant history which he had been taught.

He then handed me a small volume entitled: "Plain Reasons Why You Should Not Join The Church Of Rome." by the Reverend Canon Littledale, a contemporary of Cardinal Newman, who remained in the Church of England. I hurried home with this book thinking here, at last, would be an easy way out of my perplexity. But to my dismay, I discovered that each of the reasons proposed was based on assumed doctrine or practice which I already knew to be hopelessly distorted from the truth. I have always regretted that I did not secure a copy of this book. It helped me to find the truth and, with proper guidance, it would help others to see how misinterpretation of the truth, no matter how free from malice the author may be, can be just as deadly as if it stemmed directly from Satan. But failing that, I hope to show how deadly even a little misinterpretation can be. Then we will have done with Apologetics and turn ourselves to the enjoyment of some of the more happy treasures of our Faith.

Study Questions:

1. Comment on G. K. Chesterton's words about the appraisal of Christianity and show its application to Catholicism.

2. Show how the term "Protestant", while invented only in recent centuries, applies to the behaviour of dissidents throughout the history of the Church.

3. What is the Promise of Christ which is said to secure the perpetuity of the Catholic Church?

4. Explain the common misunderstanding of the Doctrine of Infallibility.

5. Explain the true meaning of the Doctrine of Infallibility and comment on its necessity.

6. Comment on the status of the Blessed Virgin Mary among Protestants in general.

7. Discuss the effect of bad example from within the Church.

8. Describe the author's struggle to reconcile the Divinity of Christ with what seemed like the failure of Christ's promise regarding His Church and discuss the non-Catholic's answers which deny the failure of the promise.

9. Discuss the alternative of admitting the failure of the Promise of Christ regarding His Church.

10. Describe the author's trek through this maze of conflicting possibilities.

CHAPTER V

CHRIST'S DIVINITY:
THE CORNERSTONE OF FAITH

It has long been dinned into my ears that: "Nobody will listen to you if you talk seriously. You have to make it light and easy." I hope, however, that this is not universally true. There are some things that are so serious that they simply do not make sense if they are tossed about in a trivial manner.

The matter of this chapter is *the* most serious subject there is! It is the very object of all the precedes and all that follows: *Christ's divinity, the cornerstone of faith.* Divine Faith is nothing else but union with the will of Christ as God. And so it is the answer to the petition: "Thy will be done on earth as it is in heaven."

But it is, first and always, a love-story and so it is lightsome, no matter how it is treated. "God so loved the world that He gave His Only Begotten Son, in order that whoever believes in Him should not perish, but possess eternal life." (John 3:16, Spencer). If I were able, I would sing this love-song or play it on a musical instrument. But failing that, I shall ask Christ to play it upon your hearts. In so doing He may remind you of the words of Saint Paul: "We are ambassadors therefore on behalf of Christ, as though God were entreating by us. We implore you, on behalf of Christ to be reconciled to God! ... And as His co-workers we entreat you not to receive the grace of God in vain: for He says: "At an acceptable time I listened to thee, and in a day of salvation I succored thee. Behold, now is the 'acceptable time'; behold, now is the 'day of salvation.'" (II Cor. 5:20-6:2).

To know that Christ is God is so stupendous that it lends itself to disbelief. In fact, it is completely beyond the realm of reason chiefly because it is such an infinite act of love!

We do not need the scientist to tell us what an infinitesimal speck of dust this world is compared with the universe we can see. Nor do we need him to remind us that the sojourn of man upon the earth is an infinitesimal moment, compared with the time that we can perceive. Still less, however, do we need him to interpret for us the insinuation that this nothingness of man makes nonsense out of the assertion that the world was made for man, or that it makes blasphemy of the notion that the Creator of it all became Man and that, supposing that He did become Man, He would allow these worthless mites of His creation to nail Him to a tree.

To such doubters, we might quote the reminder which Saint Paul gave to the Jews of Antioch who repelled his teaching: "Take care therefore, that what is said in the Prophets may not come upon you: 'Behold, you scorners, and wonder and vanish away! For I will do a work in your days, a work which you would by no means believe, were one to relate it to you.'" (Acts 13:40-31). Yes, it is impossible, humanly impossible to conceive, and yet it is true. It would make blasphemy for our very thought to imagine it — if it had not happened!

And that is precisely why it happened the way it did. God is so far beyond us that His love is incomprehensible to us. His act of love was so far beyond the comprehension of the purely natural intellect of man that man called it blasphemy, and so *did* nail Him to the Cross. "Then the High Priest tore his robe exclaiming: 'He has blasphemed. What further need have we for witnesses? Why, now you have heard the blasphemy. What is your opinion?' 'He deserves death.' was their answer." (Matt. 26:65).

And so the generosity of this immense act of love of God for us, which would be impossible to imagine, and is indeed hard to believe, *is* the very thing that makes it necessary for us to believe – nay, more; to know for certain. That is why we should approach with love and good will the examination of the evidence to be found in the New Testament. I say "goodwill" because there are many now-a-days who consider themselves Christians who never really seek that necessary conviction. They are content to coast along without ever thinking of the stake they have at issue. They are easily misled by those who actively deny the evidence.

All through the centuries, from the Scribes and Pharisees of the Jewish Sanhedrin, down to the Modernists and Rationalists and self-styled Higher Critics of today, the all-but-impossible mystery of the Incarnation – the Word-taking-flesh, has been a stumbling-block that either has to be believed with utter reliance upon the word of God, or else rejected with a bitterness that characterizes unaided reason in the face of mystery.

And why is this true? For reasons similar to those for which it was so bitterly denied by the Chief Priests and Scribes and Pharisees when it was first claimed by Christ Himself. Chief of which is this: If Christ is God, then His teaching and the record of His teaching cannot be false. But His teaching demands complete reorientation of men's lives founded on love, humility, obedience, abandonment to the will of God, self-sacrifice, acceptance of suffering.

True, Christ offered inducements for belief which seem to us to be irresistible. We cannot see why all men are not impressed by the appeal expressed by Saint Paul: "I hold that the sufferings of the present time bear no comparison to the glory which is to be revealed in us." (Rom. 8-18).

We stand amazed that many seem to consider the price too high for a reward so great. We do not stop to recall that appreciation of the reward usually *follows* belief instead of causing it.

There is a danger, however, in taking for granted the divinity of Christ in the sense of being casual about it, which many do not realize. The danger is this: If one does not know for sure why it is possible to declare the doctrine with such certainty, there is danger to their faith when they are brought into close contact with the large throng of so-called sophisticated people who speak of and think of the Gospel story as "The Christian Myth".

In other words, many call themselves Christian because it is socially convenient to hold that name. But at the same time, with casual indifference, or even with deliberate malice, they deny the only fact which makes Christianity mean anything, namely; that Jesus of Nazareth is God.

Believers sometimes lose sight of the fact that this is perhaps the only absolutely necessary doctrine of Christian faith. What I mean is this: Christ, Who is God, founded His Church and gave us what we call "The Deposit of Faith". It is all equally true, since it is the word of God. Being God, however, He might have made every doctrine different from what it is, except that one — that Jesus of Nazareth is God. If He be not God, then all the rest is meaningless. Our Faith is nonsense and we are, as Saint Paul says: "of all men the most pitiable." (I Cor. 15:17).

Most converts to the Catholic Faith are actively aware of the importance of this attitude of mind because not one of them would be a Catholic unless one of two possible convictions had taken possession of their soul: either, from not believing, they had begun to believe that Christ is God and had followed that conviction to its logical conclusion; or, from believing that Christ is God, they had come to see that a denial of the Catholic Church is impossible for them because, if the Catholic Church is false, Christ's promise to the contrary, regarding *His* Church, has failed; if the record that He *made* such a promise is false, then Christ has allowed us to be deceived. In either case, Christ cannot be God, since God cannot deceive or be deceived.

Not long ago I became aware for the first time that the Jehovah's Witnesses of today deny the divinity of Christ on the ground that it is not proved in the Bible.

Having this in mind, and knowing that the Jehovah Witness denial is based on the principle that Christ only claimed to be the Son of God, without reference to divinity, I did some careful scrutinizing in my last reading of the New Testament. I took care to note all the passages which prove that Christ claimed to be God, or show that He proved that He was God. Thus I omitted all those passages which prove Him to be the Son of God in a sense which could be other than divine.

The result is really quite surprising. I have always known that the evidence in Holy Scripture of the revelation of Christ's divinity is plentiful, but I have previously had a tendency to admit that perhaps it is not compelling. But after finding forty-two texts in the Gospels alone, it is difficult for me to understand how anyone can read the New Testament as it is ordinarily translated into English, and refuse to admit the certainty of the revelation of the divinity of Jesus of Nazareth.

Let us examine some of the texts that seem to offer no alternative between belief and arbitrary refusal to believe. Probably the most unequivocal statement of the fact is found in the first chapter of the Gospel according to St. John. This text contains the key to the purpose of the entire Gospel, namely; to prove that Christ is God.

St. John's opening sentence is as follows: "In the beginning was the Word, and the Word was with God, and *the Word was God...*" He then amplifies the certainty that the Word was God, and ends, in verse fourteen by saying: "And the Word became flesh and dwelt among us." Whatever else may be said of this passage of Scripture, there can be no doubt as to what knowledge St. John intended to convey to his readers!

There are really only two alternatives to the acceptance of this text as a final and conclusive proof. Both have been proposed. The first is called the "kenotic" theory and suggests that, in becoming Man, the Word abdicated His divinity for the duration of His life upon earth. The second simply denies that the New Testament is true precisely because it proves that Christ is true God and true Man. The denial of the authenticity of the New Testament has already been dealt with in our Chapter three. Arbitrary refusal to believe in the divinity of Christ has been shown to be at the root of most of the attacks against it.

There are two ways of refusing to believe. They are characteristic of all of the denials of the divinity of Christ in the face of the mystery of the Incarnation. Being unable to explain *how* a thing is true, some men refuse to believe *that* it is true. Now, a mystery does not imply that a truth is secret or obscure or doubtful. It simply means that it is beyond the reach of the human intellect to understand the "how" of a fact that God has revealed to be true.

So, understanding now the meaning of "mystery", let us take a look at Christ's own revelation and proof of His divinity. Here is an equal wealth of material but one occasion stands out above all others, both for definiteness and for impossibility of misinterpretation. It is the account of His trial before the Jewish Sanhedrin, reported in each of the Gospels, at which, under oath, He, to quote the Jews themselves, "Made Himself out to be God." (Matt. 26:53-65; Mark 14:61; Luke 22:70; John 10:30 and 19:7). And, instead of modifying the claim when, for that sole reason, they declared Him guilty of death, He allowed it to be reaffirmed by the Jews when they took Him before Pontius Pilate on the following day. This is the most convincing proof of Christ's own claim to be God, because it is made under oath, before the constituted authority, and because it was made deliberately under certain pain of death by crucifixion.

Another example, no less emphatic, of Christ's claim to be God, is even more complete, because it was immediately accompanied by a miraculous proof. It is found in the instantaneous cure of a paralytic in the presence of a hostile group of Pharisees, reported by Matthew, Mark and Luke. (Matt. 9:1-8; Mark 2:1-12 and Luke 5:17-26). Here Jesus deliberately prepared the case by laying Himself open to the hostile challenge of claiming to be God. Instead of curing the man at once, He said: "Man, thy sins are forgiven thee," (Luke 5:21) knowing that the Jews would immediately lend themselves to His purpose by stating His claim themselves. This they did by saying: "Who can forgive sins but God alone?" (Luke 5:22). Whereupon Jesus used their words to declare an unanswerable proof that He *was* "God alone" by saying to the paralytic: "I say to thee: Rise! take up thy cot and go home."

Many more direct proofs by Christ Himself that He was true God are found in these three "Synoptic" Gospels. And St. John tells us, first and last, that the sole purpose of his Gospel is: "that you may believe that Jesus is the Christ, the Son of God, and that believing, you may have *life* in His Name." (John 20:31).

But why go on multiplying quotations from Scripture? The evidence is so positive and so abundant that it must be accepted and believed with amazement, gratitude and wonder, or it must be rejected with hate and suspicion on grounds other than those that are natural and obvious.

The culminating proof of Christ's Divinity and the substantiation of all the other proof which He furnished during His whole life, was His own Crucifixion and Resurrection, all the events of which were planned and directed by Himself as He foretold in detail. This was witnessed by His disciples and even by His very executioners themselves. When they were informed of the Resurrection by their own watchmen, they bribed them to silence instead of raising a hue and cry to recover the body as they surely would have done had they not believed their guards.

Those who take their places today do the same thing by denying all scriptural proof, not because its credentials are doubtful, but because it contains the proof of what they refuse to believe.

These proofs of the Resurrection of Christ are sometimes scornfully set aside. Even some Catholic writers allow themselves to be daunted. One of them expresses it thus: "There was a time, and not so long ago, when the Resurrection was used by the Christian apologist to prove Christ's divinity. *It was a strange aberration.* ... People will accept the Resurrection *only if they already believe in the Divinity.* The divinity supports the Resurrection, not vice versa."

Webster defines the word *aberration* as "a disorder of the mind; a deviation from what is right, natural or normal." Such a contemptuous word is a bit harsh to classify those who consider the evidence for the Resurrection of Christ the most cogent proof of His Divinity. But that is trivial compared with the glee with which Satan will take the word out of context and broadcast it to the world on the lips of the host of present-day atheists, agnostics and scorners of religion.

The Divinity of Christ is a supernatural fact. All of the evidence stands on the boundary between the natural and the supernatural. The evidence for the Resurrection is not one whit different from the rest of the evidence as to its credibility. It all requires an act of supernatural Faith for its final acceptance. This reversal as regards the Resurrection lends itself to the scorners who affirm that the simple, uneducated men who were Christ's disciples were easily deceived into imagining what they wished to believe. But no thoughtful reader of the Gospels who believes that the Evangelists wrote at least what they saw as eye witnesses, can fail to observe that the very contrary is true. Even the Apostles themselves were so slow to believe and had to have so many repetitions of compelling proofs before they finally became convinced, that they have provided posterity with a record which is practically impossible to "water-down". The record is so overwhelming that it simply demands belief or flat, arbitrary rejection as an abominable crime of deception. The Risen Christ must be loved and believed or hated and rejected. He cannot be rationally ignored as so many are attempting to do today.

That is why I have prolonged the defense of the revelation made by Christ of the truth of His Divinity. This truth must be embedded in our consciousness as the very cornerstone of our Faith − the very passport to that conviction which ties us to Him who has called us to share in the riches He has bought for us. We must be freed from that bitter fruit of rebellion which breeds the indifference manifesting itself in the world today. We must stand out from the crowd who now take for granted the Christmas Holidays with no regard for the c-h-r-i-s-t in Christmas or the h-o-l-i in Holidays.

For them it is just a festive season when business is good, friends are jovial, parties are frequent, good food and drink is abundant and everybody expects to take a good deal of time off from work and to receive quite a little loot when the presents are distributed.

For us there should indeed be an atmosphere of joyous celebration, because it commemorates the most joyous event in all of history, but it should be a celebration in adoration of the goodness of God who has forever graced mankind with an invitation to participate in His Godhood by sharing with us our manhood.

And why should I be bringing this message to you? Because the same God-Man whom I ask you to adore, laid His hands on His chosen Apostles and gave them the power and the command to bring this message to all men. These men passed on this power and this command to the man who placed his hands on my head and asked God to give me, by virtue of the blessing of the Holy Spirit, the same power and the same command to go out into the hostile world and save by love and example the victims of that enemy who, like a roaring lion, still wanders through the world seeking whom he may devour.

He said: "Go therefore, and make disciples of all nations, teaching them to observe all whatever I have commanded you: and lo, I am with you all days, even until the consummation of the world." (Matt. 28:18-20).

This promise of Christ's constant presence in His Church is coupled with a command and a delegation of authority. It becomes therefore, God's solemn covenant with all men of all time that there will be a "Deposit Of Faith" which contains all the knowledge revealed by God as to what men must know and what they must do to conform to the will of God. By the guarantee of God Himself, then, this Deposit Of Faith is to be made available to all men through the Church which He founded upon St. Peter.

The same God-Man who said to the Apostles: "He who hears you hears Me," addressed these same words, through them, to me and to you. And the same God-Man has given the same command to me which inspired St. Paul to say: "We are ambassadors therefore on behalf of Christ, as though God were entreating by us. We implore you, on behalf of Christ, to be reconciled to God!" (II Cor. 5:20). "For you now know the generosity of our Lord Jesus Christ – that though rich, He became poor for

your sakes, that by His poverty you might be made rich."
(II Cor. 8:9).

Study Questions:

1. Comment on the *importance* of the title of this chapter.

2. Comment on the agnostic scientist's assertion of the impossibility of the title of this chapter and illustrate it by citing the behavior of the rulers of the Jews.

3. Discuss the reasons for the notion of opposition to the fact of Christ's Divinity and the reasons for attraction to it.

4. What is the danger of being casual about conviction as to Christ's Divinity?

5. State the status of converts to Catholicism with reference to the Divinity of Christ?

6. Comment on the claim of Jehovah's Witnesses with respect to the Divinity of Christ.

7. Discuss the opening verses of St. John's Gospel as evidence of Christ's Divinity and mention the two answers of denial of this evidence.

8. Give two examples of Christ's own claim to be God.

9. Discuss the evidence of Christ's Resurrection as proof of His Divinity and comment on the assertion that it is not acceptable as proof.

10. Give a brief summation of the message brought to you in this chapter.

CHAPTER VI
THE MOTIVE FOR FAITH:
CATHOLIC AND NOT CATHOLIC

The Second Vatican Council has encouraged the entire Christian world to pray and work for the reunion of Christendom. It has recalled to men's minds the ardent prayer of Christ Himself when He was about to leave the world: *"I ask not only for them, but also for those who believe in Me through their word, that they may all be one; that, as Thou, Father art in Me, and I am in Thee, they also may be one in us, in order that the world may believe that Thou hast sent Me."* And indeed that last clause would be realized *if* all Christians were one!

For obvious reasons, however, Christ's prayer for unity is far from being realized among non-Catholics. But among Catholics of every race and nation it has become a uniformly accepted responsibility to pray and work for what one of the Protestant observers at the Second Session of the Council called a "second miracle of grace"; namely, the manifestation by Catholics that they do possess the One, Holy, Catholic, Apostolic Church founded by Christ.

And now that the Council has opened the way for a special grace for all Christians, all men should respond to this prayer of Christ and rekindle their acceptance of a responsibility to work and pray for reunion. But in order that our prayer and work may be well directed, we should all be aware of the nature of this "second miracle" for which non-Catholics wait and Catholics hope.

The need for a miracle stems from an essential difference between the Catholic motive for faith and that of every other Christian person. It is axiomatic to the true Catholic that Christianity does not offer a variety of choices. Christ promised a Church which would be one in Faith, one in worship, one in Sacraments from its beginning until the end of time. It would be made so by the continuous, divine, infallible protection against the forces of alteration or destruction which Christ called "The Gates Of Hell". Either we have this Church in the twentieth century, or, for a Catholic, Christianity is a tragic myth.

But here is the hitch and the necessity for a miracle: not a single member of the non-Catholic Christian world can admit this axiomatic statement because it would involve the denial of the authenticity of his own belief. One cannot logically be a non-Catholic Christian unless he believes that the Catholic Church does not fulfill the promises of Christ. And since the Catholic Church is the only one that even claims to fulfill all of these promises, he must maintain that the promises of Christ are not fulfilled in the world today. It is for this important reason that I have chosen to entitle this chapter: THE MOTIVE FOR FAITH: CATHOLIC AND NOT CATHOLIC.

Every human being in the world is a child of God. As St. Paul puts it very aptly: "He is not far from any one of us; it is in Him that we live and move and have our being." (Acts 17:28). But in his *access* to God, every human being in the world is in one of two great classes; those who have the Catholic *motive* for faith, and those who do not. Among those who do not have the Catholic motive for faith, there is the widest possible range of ideas about God and His dealings with men. All of these people, however, derive their ideas in the same manner;

namely, by means of human judgment regarding all of the evidence presented to their minds.

The savage who has no contact with the outside world draws his ideas about God from his observation of nature. He can rely on his reason to tell him a good deal about the necessity for an all-powerful Creator of things as they are.

Among those who have access to all of the accumulated knowledge and history of what we call the "civilized" world, the judgment of reason covers another wide range. What might be called the lowest concept for the reason for man's existence is based on a deliberate turning away from the philosophic notion that the world as it is demands an uncreated First Cause, and the gratuitous substitution of the only alternative – the stupendous miracle of the self-existence of all that is. The Atheist or Materialist can have no other basis for his belief, even though he is forced to admit that what he calls the highest form of matter – which is himself – has no control whatever over its own existence as such, nor does it have any direct control over the life principle of its body.

Advancing away, however, from that rather strange materialistic product of reason, the concept of God and religion has, perhaps, almost as many forms as there are individuals who consider the evidence. One might say that these concepts range from the materialist's *zero*, up to the individual who might believe everything that the Catholic Church teaches because it satisfies his reason. He is not a Catholic because he fears the possibility that the Catholic Church might, in the future, teach as "of faith" something which his reason might not choose to accept.

This man may have a neighbor who believes *almost* all that the Catholic Church teaches, but as to certain teaching of the Church his reason tells him that it cannot come from God because his human judgment refuses to accept it.

Next, we come to those who have the Catholic motive for faith. This, unfortunately, does *not* include all who call themselves Catholics, because one who has the true Catholic motive for faith would not become lukewarm or fall away, nor would he publicly inveigh against the teaching of the Holy Father as so many do today.

This *true* Catholic motive for faith also begins with a consideration of the evidence to be found in the world around us and the evidence of history. It becomes *Catholic*, however, only when it steps from the natural to the supernatural by an act of the free-will, aided by help from God. It is not accepted item-by-item merely because it accommodates itself to human reason. It is by this gift from God that one is made to understand that God, the Creator of the universe, has given to the human race an absolutely certain means of knowing all that one needs to know to enable him to obey God, to worship Him and to reach eternal life in the manner which has been ordained by God.

God did this in a way which was utterly unimaginable. He, the Creator of the universe, assumed human nature and became the God-man, Jesus of Nazareth. He proved beyond doubt that He was God and then made certain promises which would, to put it mildly, be quite impossible to believe had they not come directly from God!

Of these promises, the one which constitutes the Catholic's present motive for faith, is that He, God, would provide the world throughout all time, with a body of men who would be protected by His supernatural power so that they would make known with infallible certainty all that Jesus had revealed to His Apostles in Person, without change, error or omission. He would also give them supernatural guidance which would enable them to protect this deposit of faith and, by means of it, to teach, govern and sanctify all men until the end of the world. This promised guarantee of God, therefore, takes into account all of the development of knowledge, of history, and of science in every age.

This means that the Catholic form of worship, the doctrine and the pattern of moral behavior, is believed today solely because it is guaranteed as well as commanded by almighty God. One having the true Catholic motive for faith knows that there can be no possibility that he will ever find himself in the dilemma which I have mentioned with respect to his neighbor who fears that he may not always agree with the teaching of the Catholic Church. To the true Catholic, this would be nonsense because it would amount to saying: "I might not always agree with God."

To understand this situation somewhat better, then, let us imagine a conversation with a non-Catholic who is unwilling to risk committing himself to truth about God which is beyond the capacity of his human power of reason. This imaginary conversation will occupy the remainder of this chapter and might be somewhat as follows:

"Let us look at your individual position in regard to this general observation about the motive for faith. You say: 'I cannot stop myself from thinking and I know that if I should become a Catholic I would go on having the same thoughts and it would be hypocritical to say that I did not.'

"In answer to that, let us for the moment suppose the impossible; let us suppose that you had a vision which gave you utter certainty that it came from God, and you were told in this vision that you could go to a certain room at any time and there get an explanation directly from God of any proposition that was presented to you that you found difficult to reconcile with the answer you had arrived at by the use of reason.

"At first, you might be a little hesitant to take full advantage of this precious privilege because it would seem too good to be true. But, if you tentatively tried it out a few times and found that it worked perfectly every time, and the answers were infallible proof against any argument that could be posed against them, all your hesitancy would vanish. You would be utterly grateful to God and would look forward to the rest of your life without any anxiety as to your ability and desire to be submissive to the will of God, and to give Him exactly the kind of worship and love and obedience that He might make known to you in the future as being His will.

"You would even accept gladly explanations from God that might be quite the opposite of ideas concerning which you had expressed yourself in the past to other men. That would not involve any humiliation because you would know definitely that you had been wrong before. Perhaps your former error had occurred because you had arrived at certain conclusions that were perfectly sound conclusions as to the arguments that led to them, but now you learned that the arguments themselves were untenable because they opposed the positive law of God. You would believe this even though you might not be able to see quite why God should make such a law. You would, therefore, have no difficulty in revising your thinking to make it conform to God's will.

"Suppose again, that you get into the habit of going to this private place where God is accustomed to speak to you, so that you go there very frequently. Your reason for going has changed somewhat. To be sure, you go every time you have any difficulty that needs an answer, but you often go just to tell God how grateful you are for this privilege and to express your love and adoration for God, which is growing by leaps and bounds.

"Suppose once more, that one day you were to go to this place and God would say to you: 'My son, I am not altogether pleased with you because you have not yet let this special privilege which I have given you bring you to see that all the information which I have given to you

directly, has always been available to you just as certainly
from Me, but conveyed by the human voices of men
whom I, by My divine power, have made My instruments
to tell you My will. You have always taken the attitude
that the answers they could give you were simply the
result of positing their power of reasoning against your
power of reasoning, and that it would be not only humili-
ating but beneath the dignity of your human nature to
accept their teaching on any other basis than its direct
appeal to your reason.

" 'Now, I am displeased with you on two counts: first,
because I have given evidence such that all men may
know that the men who have been chosen by Me as My
instruments are guaranteed by Me, now, in the twentieth
century. They are protected by My divine power from
giving you any false information as to the doctrine that I
wish them to teach, or the behavior that I wish you to
follow, or the kind of worship that I have a right to
expect, or the love that I wish you to have for Me as well
as for all those who are My children.

" 'I have not only given this evidence, but I have also
declared that it is sufficient. Since, however, the final step
of faith in this Teaching Authority has a supernatural
destination, it requires the help of a direct gift from Me
which is called grace. I have promised this grace to everyone who will humbly ask it of Me with submissive prayer,
trusting in Me in spite of every obstacle, just as Abraham
trusted in Me when I asked him to sacrifice his son, Isaac,
to Me.

" 'This promise of grace, however, does not mean that
you are to be relieved by grace from the necessity of a
free act of your human will. You must, as it were, use
your natural free will to step from the natural world into
the supernatural world. True, you could not do it without
supernatural help for the very reason that it is a step *into*
a means of knowing in which I am a Partner and is, therefore, as the word *supernatural* says, *above* the capacity of

your nature to achieve without Me. But, not only is it a step *into*, but also, and first, it is a *step*. The destination of the step is supernatural and so requires My help. The step itself must be your free act because I have decreed that it must be free. *You* must be willing to take the step, not because of My compulsion, but because you trust Me, and trusting Me you love Me. Your love compelled would be hateful to Me; your love seeking Me is the reason for which I have created this world. Your step is natural; My help is supernatural; they must occur precisely together to terminate in the kind of faith which would generate the love to make your soul the kind of dwelling-place where I and My Son wish to make our abode.

" 'And that, My son, brings up the second count upon which I am somewhat displeased with you. Let us face it, your reluctance toward acceptance of the means which I have provided for you to know My will, has been justified by you, along with millions of other men who still hold back from Me on the ground that it is beneath human dignity to accept any doctrine that one cannot feel convinced of directly as a result of the argument presented to his reason. Now, human reason without supernatural aid, can take one no farther than the evidence presented to him through his senses. But the spiritual world and the supernatural world is beyond the reach of the senses. And so, for that matter, is a very large part of the truth concerning things in the physical world — existence, for example — and life. These things are in the realm of My infinite knowledge and My infinite power.

" 'To demand from My human instruments a proof entirely within the reach of your reason is to exercise a degree of pride which is far beyond the just demand of a human soul which can know that it is utterly dependent upon Me for its existence and for its power of reason and for its eternal destiny. It is the same pride that has kept men from understanding the depth of My love since

Adam was persuaded by Satan to say: "God knows that if we eat of this tree of knowledge we will be like Him, knowing good and evil."

" 'It is the same pride in the hearts of many men today who vaunt their status as members of the human race which places them above the dignity of every other being in the created material world. They are blinded by the fact that the sole reason for their dignity is that I have given them that godlike faculty of intelligence and free-will so that they have in their hearts the knowledge of the behavior fitting to their nature and can choose whether they will honor that law of their nature or will betray it and defile it. They allow themselves to be blinded to the fact that the reason they have dignity is precisely because they are *not* like beasts which I have not given free-will or knowledge, but only instinct, which causes them to have only the urges and appetites which bring about the ends for which I have created them. Acting in this blindness, these men degrade the precious appetite for procreation which I have not bound in men as I have in beasts, so that the urge is limited to the end for which it is given.

" 'Instead, they make themselves lower than unknowing beasts and pierce My Heart anew, day after day, with words and actions which defy this law of their nature which I have attached to the sacred bond of marriage. Not only do they insult Me by their abuse of My gift of free-will, but, boasting of it, they set themselves up against My holiness in multiple sins of scandal by which weak souls are given a vestige of encouragement in sin and others are invited to add to the scandal by acquiescence and silence.

" 'And so it is today! As a penalty for the malice of those who close their hearts to this law of their nature, there comes a blindness which numbs their minds against it, even though I have caused My prophets to remind them that — "I will implant My law in their inmost thoughts, engrave it in their hearts." (Jer. 31:33 Knox). And so it sometimes takes a still more evil form in the willed and deliberate murder of an unborn child because they do not trust My Providence for its mother, or because *they* decide for the child that it would rather be deprived of life and heaven than risk a deformed body, or just because it would be too much trouble to become the parents of another child. When I have created an immortal soul and united it to a budding human body, it becomes a person who has rights which also belong to Me. It is helpless and has injured no one. How would you like to stand before My Judgment-Seat and offer these reasons for taking its life?

" 'This frame of mind toward Me is not natural to men. It is the penalty of selfishness and pride and malice. When self-love is allowed, by little and little, to take possession of men's souls, they become expert in devising ways to shut Me out of their minds. I have given you a prayer which acknowledges the majesty of My kingdom over heaven and earth. In that prayer, I have taught men to say: "Thy will be done on earth as it is in heaven." This petition is meant for men, not for Me. Be assured, My will *is* done on earth! Men *could* make it done on earth as it is in heaven by cooperating with the grace which I offer them. But when they close their minds against Me, I withdraw that grace. It is then that they enforce *their* will by making it unlawful for little children in their schools to ask Me for this grace so that My will may be done on earth *as* it is in heaven. These children, too, will grow up into men and women who will refuse My dominion over them. Remember, however, "God is not mocked! " (Gal. 6:7).

" 'It is for you, then to *join in prayer* with those who beg Me day and night to stay My hand in judgment of the crimes of men. It is for those precious souls who do give themselves to Me that I tolerate the present evil in the world.

" 'And so it is with all the law of man's nature as well as the positive law of love which I have revealed and have given My divine promise that it shall not fail until the end of time. No, My son, it is not priest or pope that guards the revelation which I have made known; it is My Holy Spirit dwelling in the souls of these men who are My instruments. It is He who makes known to you My will and My desire that you should enter in and share My love in the Sacraments which I have provided for you and without which you cannot belong to Me. You are indeed free to choose, but your good works will be empty and will not please Me unless you are willing to trust Me and My word.

" 'Remember this, moreover, your human reason will always pose objections after you leave My presence. You will not arrive at the conviction which I am asking of you unless you choose to set aside your individual human court-of-appeal and turn instead to Me with humble submissive trust. It is that trust in Me which leads the will to that free act which I reward with true supernatural faith from which springs the love which is dear to My Heart. When once I have given that faith, the same trust in Me must guard it all life long!

" 'It is trust which abandons itself to My will which furnished the motive for the true Catholic Faith with which I have blessed the world. If you will accept My word for this, I will flood your soul with a grace that will make you stand in awe and make you wonder how it has been possible that it has taken you so long to understand My love for you and to become united to Me in the Blessed Sacrament of My love! ' "

Study Questions:

1. What was the essential objective of Christ's own prayer for unity of Christians?

2. Explain the urge toward unity of Faith witnessed by a non-Catholic observer at the Council and the "hitch" that calls for a miracle for its accomplishment.

3. Explain how people who do not have the Catholic motive for Faith derive their ideas about God and religion and apply your answer to the savage having no contact with the outside world.

4. Discuss the variations in Faith among those who have access to all the accumulated knowledge and history of the world.

5. Explain the Catholic motive for Faith and tell what is the application of the sentence, "I might not always agree with God."

6. Elaborate the set-up imagined by the author in his assumed conversation with a non-Catholic doubter.

7. Describe the imagined reproof from God to the non-Catholic beneficiary of His words and tell the "first count" of God's displeasure.

8. Describe the "second count" of God's displeasure over the response of the non-Catholic doubter.

9. Elaborate God's explanation of the responsibility involved in man's possession of intelligence and free will and apply it to violations of God's "natural law" in contraception and abortion.

10. Elaborate the advice God gives to the doubter to enable him to arrive at the conviction God asks of him.

CHAPTER VII

GRACE: GOD'S GIFT "OUT OF THIS WORLD"

Are you annoyed at my frequent use of the word "grace" without an adequate explanation of its various meanings? Since it is practically impossible to discuss spiritual matters without referring to several different uses of that word, let us consider "GRACE".

Every Catholic occasionally or frequently or almost constantly has thoughts about a certain circumstance with respect to his soul which he refers to as a *"state* of grace". To most non-Catholics this expression is almost meaningless. And far too many Catholics give little thought to the importance of its meaning. It is my purpose, then, to help Catholics to know enough about grace so that they may appreciate it and may make the topic very interesting to their non-Catholic friends. For non-Catholics I hope to make the telling of it sufficiently interesting to make them ask for more. In so doing I hope to give Catholics a healthy respect for the importance of Sanctifying Grace and a very humble sense of gratitude for the Grace of Faith.

Perhaps I can best focus our attention on the reason for my purpose by telling you of an incident that was reported to me by one of my monastic confreres. The incident involves the well-known scholar and philosopher, Doctor Mortimer Adler, who was teaching philosophy and the theology of St. Thomas Aquinas at the University of Chicago. During a summer session, my friend and another

priest went together to attend a lecture given by Doctor
Adler. The title of the discourse was: "The Metaphysical
Aspect of the Eucharist".

Translated into ordinary unphilosophical English, this
title means that Doctor Adler was discussing the teaching
of St. Thomas with respect to the state of being of the
consecrated wafer of bread which Catholics believe has
been changed during the celebration of the Mass by the
supernatural phenomenon of transubstantiation so the
substance of bread has become the substance of the Body
and Blood, Soul and Divinity of Jesus Christ. Obviously,
it would be hard to find a subject of greater intimacy
with the heart of Catholic Faith. Equally obviously, it
would require a deep intellectual understanding of doctrine in order to discuss this subject with any degree of
adequacy.

After the lecture was over the speaker opened the subject for discussion and questions. One of the priests present rose and complimented the speaker on the excellence
of his presentation of the subject, remarking that he had
never heard a more forceful sermon concerning the
Blessed Sacrament of the Eucharist. "But", he continued,
"how is it possible for you, a Jew, to explain this doctrine with such understanding and still remain a Jew?"
We can imagine the electrified silence with which that
audience waited for Doctor Adler's reply. It came
promptly as follows: "Father, you are a student of St.
Thomas. Can it be possible that you have not made yourself familiar with the doctrine of St. Thomas set forth in
the first part of the same Summa, Questions 109 to 113
– the treatise on the Grace of God?"

It is not given to us to judge other men. As St. Paul
reminds us in addressing the Corinthians: "For who
among men knows the thoughts of a man, except the
spirit of man dwelling in him." (I Cor. 2:11). It is sobering, however, to recall that other Jews in other days have
furnished evidence of the terrifying fact that no amount

of knowledge of the truth will suffice for a supernatural act of faith without that priceless ingredient — the grace of God, for which one can dispose one's self by humble prayer, but which no one can demand of God.

Here I must repeat from a previous chapter St. John's report of the following scene in the Jewish Sanhedrin: "The Chief Priests and the Pharisees convoked the great Council. And they said: 'What are we about? for this man is working many miracles. If we let Him go on like this everybody will believe in Him'" (John 11:47-48). In other words, these men are plainly saying to each other: "This man has proved beyond the shadow of a doubt that He is God. He has proved it by restoring to life Lazarus of Bethany who has been dead and sealed in a tomb for four days!" How can it be possible that they do not see the folly of their own blindness? The awful answer is found in their motive implied in what follows: "And the Romans will come and take away both our place and our nation." (John 11:48). The answer is supernatural — their motive has closed the door to grace!

The same blindness and the same malice in the hearts of the same men is disclosed twice more after the crowning miracle of the Resurrection: Once when they bribed their own guards to lie about their own eye-witness testimony of the Resurrection itself; once more when they again convened the Council when St. Peter was brought before them for working a miracle "by the Name of Jesus Christ, The Nazarene". (Acts 4:10).

After they had ordered Peter out of their hearing, they said to each other: "What shall we do with these men? for that a notable miracle has been done through them is manifest to all the inhabitants of Jerusalem, and we cannot deny it."

Again, how is it possible for the very men who say these words to deny the only answer that makes sense? The answer which again is supernatural should have prompted them to adore Him as God whom they had crucified as a malefactor. There is no escape from the awful conclusion that their blindness is the just punishment for their proud resistance to the external grace of miracles which they themselves had testified as authentic.

Father Andres Fernandez helps us to understand this fearsome concomitant of malice. He says: "Christ constantly tried to enlighten and convince these, His implacable enemies. Obviously, He could have given them internal graces which would have moved their wills, but He did not, and who will dare to call Him to account for His mode of action? Here we touch upon that profound mystery of Divine Providence and grace, which we are not allowed to penetrate," but which should remind us to seek God's help with fear as well as with gratitude. (Life of Christ, p. 375).

It is now high time to return to the purpose of this chapter and explain the various uses of the word "grace". I have already used the word with three quite different meanings which are vital to our understanding of these dramatic tragedies which I have cited as connected with its misdirection.

Not long ago I read an article warning priests not to use difficult words in their sermons without defining them. The article stated that of twenty-five educated adults asked to explain the spiritual meaning of the word "grace", only one knew that it had any other meaning than that of a prayer said before meals. We, however, are obviously not concerned with this use of the word. The grace which interests us is a supernatural gift of help available only in a transaction or series of transactions with almighty God.

The ultimate goal of all other graces is the achievement of "sanctifying" or "habitual" grace. Its importance and its special character make it desirable that it be explained first. The other meanings will then explain themselves.

The Latin expression for Sanctifying Grace is "gratia sanctificans". This, literally translated, means: saint-

making gift or favor. That really explains it better than
any other brief definition could. It means a state resulting
from the infusion into the soul of a supernatural quality
which makes one a friend of God and makes one's acts of
virtue into tokens of that friendship. It gives one the
capacity to become a saint whereas without it there is no
possibility of sainthood howsoever holy one's life may appear to be.

Sanctifying Grace gives a permanent state to a soul
unless by a direct act of enmity toward God, it is driven
out by grave sin. I say "it" is driven out, "It" is not the
proper word to use. I should say, God is driven out, since
that is precisely what happens when sin deprives a soul of
Sanctifying Grace. Just as natural birth starts one out
with all the nascent equipment to become a rational
human being, so the infusion of Sanctifying Grace, which
is part of the spiritual re-birth of Baptism, equips the soul
for divine life which culminates in the complete possession of God in heaven.

God is present in the not-yet-glorified soul of a way-
farer such as we are, somewhat as the intellect is present
in an infant. God's presence there is just as real. That is
why we can truly say that a soul possessing Sanctifying
Grace is a true temple of the Holy Spirit of God. So it
should be easy to see that the loss of this treasure is a far
greater calamity than anything else that can befall a
human being. It is far greater than the loss of property or
health or even life itself.

Sanctifying Grace, however, differs from the natural
qualities of a soul, in that it can be lost. When one receives Sanctifying Grace in his soul, four things happen at
the same instant: God takes up His presence in the soul;
the soul turns toward God with a gift of supernatural
faith; it turns away from sin with detestation; and the
detested sins are remitted.

It is impossible to over-emphasize the preciousness of
the possession of Sanctifying Grace in one's soul. Tan-

query, the great master of the spiritual life, spends pages of his treatise devising expressions and comparisons to try to make its richness reach the core of our hearts, but no finite comparison begins to be adequate for the very reason that the infusion of Sanctifying Grace into a soul is a truly deifying light. It is to the soul what the soul is to the body, namely, a life-principle.

This divine life-principle gives the soul a participation in the divine nature, not indeed a substantial union as in the Person of Christ, true God and true Man, but none the less a true participation. This indwelling presence of God places in the soul its participation in the divine nature, as it were, in the form of a bud, or a seed, or the image of a seal in wax.

The analogy of the bud gives the best hint of reality. It can constantly grow and increase in fragrance and beauty even though it cannot in this life reach its ultimate form of the flower of Beatific Vision. Yet all the time it remains subject to the possibility of being snatched away or destroyed by the dry, hot blast of our lower nature leading to grave sin. Again, it can become withered or starved by lesser sin.

On the other hand, its growth and fragrance are nourished by the perfection and simplicity of our faith. This supernatural gift of faith is nothing less than the pure light of God's glory shining on the soul, imperfectly receptive to be sure, because limited by the imperfection of our finiteness. Yet, this grace of faith, helped by God and enriched by the active cooperation of our free-will, will cause that bud to come nearer and nearer to the perfect flower of Beatific Vision of God as He is in Himself.

This prepares the soul for eternal union and possession of God when our mortality, finally permeated with the light of glory and freed from imperfection, reflects this true and deifying Light of the World-to-Come. It is only then that we will reap the benefit of our careful cultivation of the bud of this flower all the days of our life upon earth. It is only then that we will appreciate the loving admonition given us by God during every hour of our life in this world and solemnly taught us by St. Paul: "Behold, *now* is the 'acceptable time; behold, *now* is the day of salvation'." (II Cor. 6:2). It is only then that we will fully appreciate the importance of every act of our life in its relation to this ineffable treasure of Sanctifying Grace in the soul.

Now, if we have begun to get even a faint notion of the importance of the possession of Sanctifying Grace in the soul, we will see that its possession and cultivation are more important than all the rest of the activities of our daily life put together. "But," you may say, "most of the activities of our daily life are matters of duty that we cannot set aside in favor of the cultivation of Sanctifying Grace." And I am glad that you put it that way, because that is the most important thing of all for us to learn in the consideration of Sanctifying Grace! Every act, every breath, every bite of food may be a means of nourishing and increasing Sanctifying Grace. St. Francis de Sales expresses it neatly by coupling two quotations from different Epistles of St. Paul. He says: "All, whatever you do in word and in work, do all in the name of Jesus Christ... Whether you eat or drink or whatever you do, do all to the glory of God." (I Cor. 10:31 and Col. 3:17). But, alas! almost every one may also be a means of blighting it or even of destroying it!

So, let us conclude by studying the ways and means, here and now, of obtaining and cultivating this pearl of great price, this bud of eternal glory, this matrix from which will spring the rivers of living water which Christ has promised: "If anyone thirsts let him come to Me and drink. He who believes in Me as the Scripture has said, out of his heart shall flow rivers of living water." (John 7:37-38).

There are four possible starting-points for beginning the quest for Sanctifying Grace: First, the unbaptized infant; second, the one who has reached the age of reason and has not learned of the promises of Christ or of the commands respecting His Church; third, the one who has received the Sacrament of Baptism, but in whom the bud has died of starvation as a result of culpable ignorance; fourth, the unfortunate soul from whom Sanctifying Grace has been driven by grave sin.

The necessary procedure to gain or re-gain this treasure of Sanctifying Grace in each of these four states can be derived from a simple knowledge of certain general facts. First and foremost, "saint-making grace" as the name implies, is a free gift from almighty God which cannot be earned by anyone *independently* of God. But this statement must immediately be coupled with the knowledge that God desires the sanctification of every soul.

How, then, if God who is omnipotent so desires, does it not follow that every soul automatically receives sanctification? The answer is that God is so jealous of that gift of free-will which He has given freely to every soul, that He demands the cooperation of our free-will with every offer of His gift of grace.

The cultivation of, or preparation for, the gift of Sanctifying Grace is by means of temporary or passing helps from God called actual graces. They are helps by which God in His mercy moves our will and yet allows us to act freely so as to cooperate. But also, by a stern act of justice, God allows our will to resist grace and so to suffer a tragic loss through our own fault.

The first condition for the health of Sanctifying Grace, as we have seen, is supernatural faith in the truths revealed by God. This faith is infused in the Baptism of an infant, together with Sanctifying Grace, in a nascent state like the other faculties of the soul. With proper parental care, grace and faith will follow as the natural faculties develop. On the other hand, with the dawn of reason, they may be neglected and die.

But even then, God offers every soul sufficient grace

to be reinstated or to gain an increase in Sanctifying Grace through acts based on faith or a first act of faith. These helps by the omniscient ingenuity of God, take every form both external and internal; the example of a friend; the conversion of another; a chance conversation or sermon or book; a crisis in one's life; the inner conviction of reason aided by internal grace and prayer; each in accordance with the needs of the individual soul. These graces invite the unbeliever to faith, the sinner to repentance, the just man to ever higher perfection. God constantly helps the free-will, but He will never compel acceptance of the help.

But once that precious treasure, that bud of sainthood, is infused into the soul, it becomes a branch of that sacred Vine freely drawing divine help from every experience of daily life, and thus bringing to perfection that flower of glory one day to bloom in the eternal sunshine of heaven!

Study Questions:

1. Comment on the author's introduction to the chapter on *Grace* and the various uses of the word.
2. Describe the incident of Dr. Adler's lecture and its connection with the consideration of *Grace*.
3. Comment on the necessity of Grace for a supernatural act of Faith as evidenced by the behavior of the Jewish Sanhedrin in three miracles.
4. Give the comment of Father Fernandez on the withdrawal of Grace in the presence of malice and his justification of God's action.
5. Explain the meaning of "Sanctifying Grace" and describe it as a "state."
6. Elaborate the supernatural status of Sanctifying Grace in the soul and compare it with the natural faculties.
7. What four things happen simultaneously when one receives Sanctifying Grace and why is it so precious?

8. Elaborate the analogy of Sanctifying Grace as a *bud* of the divine life-principle.

9. Discuss the procedure of cultivating Sanctifying Grace quoting Saint Paul.

10. Elaborate the ways and means of obtaining and cultivating Sanctifying Grace and explain the accompanying function of "actual" Graces giving examples.

CHAPTER VIII

HOPE AIMS FAITH AT CHARITY

Every missionary spends most of his life promoting the all-important theological virtue of Faith. Every Christian soul should be familiar with St. Paul's stirring eulogy of the greatest of all virtues, the theological virtue of Charity. But far too many of us overlook that indispensable hinge which anchors in Faith and opens the door of Charity — that theological virtue of Hope.

Faith and Hope are indispensable to each other. Neither can survive without the other, even though both together may survive in an attenuated form when Charity has been lost. So, while no one will deny that the greatest of the theological virtues is Charity, the prudent, earnest Christian will not be slow to sense the fact, since Charity is the flower of Faith only when it is nourished by Hope, the latter is the virtue which should merit our attention here and now in this world. In fact, it is Hope that furnishes a most worthy motive power or fuel to put Charity into every act of your daily life.

Before going further we should make clear just what is meant by the theological virtue of Hope. This is important because there are several kinds of hope, one at least, diametrically the opposite of the virtue which I am recommending.

The theological virtue of Hope is the conviction, based on Faith-in-the-Promises-of-Christ that, if one lives in conformity with the will of God, he will, with difficulty to be sure, but none the less certainly, be given that priceless gift of final perserverance and everlasting life in perfect union with God. The puny insignificance of any other aim of hope in this world makes the theological virtue of Hope incomparably superior and the only one which merits earnest effort to cultivate on the part of every Christian.

The reason that the supernatural virtues of Faith, Hope and Charity are called theological virtues, is that their direct object is God or union with God or the possession of God. So, when it is understood that every thought and word and act of every individual in this world is done or said in the intimate presence of God, it is easy to see that the individual who constantly adverts to that fact, and intentionally refers every act to God's good pleasure, is actually elevating every act to the supernatural plane. This supernatural elevation of the will makes every act supernaturally meritorious even though that explicit intention is not always present.

Of course, any act of supernatural merit presupposes a state of Sanctifying Grace in the soul and that, as we have seen, is a gift from God. Moreover, the gift of Sanctifying Grace is always accompanied by the infusion of the supernatural virtues together with the indwelling of God Himself. But all this treasure can remain fairly dormant unless one responds to that nascent spring of enthusiasm which lies in the virtue of Hope informed by Faith. That is the combination which carries with it the alchemy which has the power of transmuting every human act into the precious gold of eternal value.

Of course, this is the very reason why the virtue of Hope is neglected by so many of us. It is because its "pay day" is all in heaven. True supernatural hope is only interested in the affairs of this world insofar as they are manifestations of the will of God, or opportunities to conform to the will of God. The goal of Hope is all on the other side of the grave, or even still more remote, on the final Day of Judgment. But how stupid is our puny human choice to discard it because it seems remote. And "seems" is the word to use because, compared with eternal good, there is nothing in time that is as near or as dear.

We may think that the Bible story of Esau sounds unreal, and doubt that he actually gave up his right as heir to his father's estate for a dish of food when he was hungry. But any act of ours which sets aside, for any earthly reason, an opportunity to please God, is a far more stupid waste of our heavenly birthright. And to commit grave sin and so deliberately make ourselves God's enemies, is infinitely greater folly.

How is it possible that we can be so blind? Objectively there is no answer. Considering man in the abstract, it does not make sense that a sane human being would give up so much for so little. But, let's face it, so-called sane human beings are doing it right along — hundreds of millions of them.

In fact, there are very few of us who have not at some time made a choice equivalent to that of Esau. He came in tired from the hunt and said to his brother Jacob: "Give me of this red pottage for I am exceeding faint." And Jacob said to Him: "Sell me thy first birthright." and he answered: "Why surely, I shall have little profit of my birthright if I am to die of hunger as I stand here." "Give me thy oath," said Jacob; and Esau gave his oath and made over his birthright. And so, taking the bread and the pottage he ate and drank and went his way; making little account of having sold his first birthright. (Gen. 25:30-34).

Even lesser sin is as short-sighted as this act of Esau when we compare it with a lost opportunity to bring ourselves closer to God. And grave sin is infinitely more stupid. This could only happen to a soul in whom the virtue of Hope has been stifled. Hope can only be stifled when Faith has been stunted. Faith is stunted by the careless indifference of small sins or the malicious enmity of grave sins.

Supernatural merit is the coin which measures one's savings account in heaven. It is just as real as one's soul is real. It might be called the bonus pay that one who is in a state of grace may receive for every thought and word and act of this life when it stems from a love of God and has love for its underlying motive. And this is true even though it is thought of only occasionally. This also applies to the unimportant acts of our work or our duty or our recreation or even of our rest.

Merit accumulates all life long and draws interest up to the day of our death. The bank which stores our merit can never be subject to failure. One nickel's worth of merit is worth more than all the cash income of a lifetime. No depression can ever injure our merit account. It is perfectly safe against thieves or even against our own bad judgment because we cannot spend a dime of it until we are dead! *And* that last item makes it *more* valuable rather than less!

It is true that no merit bonus is paid for any act unless it is countersigned by supernatural love of God. And love of God does not function in this world unless it is powered by Hope. Hope is what we have when we know that these facts about merit are true. Hope is the fuel; Hope is the hinge upon which Charity hangs when Hope is anchored in Faith.

Opposed to this supernatural Hope there is, as I have said, one contemptible form of hope that is by no means entitled to the name of virtue. It is the motive such as that which inspires Communism to dominate the world and to impose on men and matter a regime of godless and hence hopeless regimentation. The advocates of this deadly travesty of Christian Hope refer to the latter as "The Opiate of Escape". While the possessor of Hope in God can see the folly of this attitude, he can also see that it is consistent with the equally fallacious premise that there is no hope outside of this material world as it is.

There is, on the other hand, a natural virtue of hope which is by no means contemptible. From this natural hope stems enthusiasm for success in worldly pursuits, all healthy ambition, ingenuity and industry as well as an ethical incentive for good behavior, such as the practice of the Golden Rule.

Let us consider an example of natural hope that is so obvious that we cannot miss the point. Suppose a young man falls in love with a young lady. If the young man is a seven-year-old and the lady is a top-ranking movie star, nothing much happens — hope lacks the necessary ingredient of possibility.

But if the young man is an eligible bachelor and the lady belongs to the family that just moved in on the next block — things are very different! Hope immediately takes command. The young man knows that it is not going to be an easy victory. In fact, there are a good many difficulties to be overcome. But there is hope! He immediately begins to spend more than a prudent amount of time devising ways and means to convince the young lady that he is just about the nicest young man she ever saw. In his own home he may be the least attractive member of the family, but around his lady-love he is unselfish, thoughtful, tactful — all because of hope. If it should turn out, however, that the lady in question is already engaged to marry a young man in her old home town, what happens? Love may linger on for a while, but hope is immediately deflated and, with the end of hope, comes the end of all the manifestation of love. There is no more joy in Johnny's plans because hope has faded away.

But, as we shall see, all the good impulses of natural hope are embraced and given much more refined incentive by the supernatural theological virtue of Hope. This incentive of supernatural Hope is infinitely greater than natural hope can ever be. The goal is never snatched away. The goodness of the goal is absolutely certain. Why is it, then, that anyone is ever slow to work at it? It can only be that it is not properly advertised. It can only be that we do not truly believe that heaven is as good or as sure as God has told us that it is. It can only be that in our short-sighted, finite human nature the virtue of Hope is neglected in favor of the puny things that attract us close at hand.

But why should this be? Is the evidence insufficient? Our whole Catholic Faith teems with proof to the contrary! But we are skeptical because it is far away and because God insists that in this life it has to be believed and cannot be seen except with the eye of Faith.

The whole Bible might be called a continuous invitation to the virtue of Hope. In fact, the entire ministry of Christ recorded in the New Testament invites one to submit to privation and persecution, hatred, insult and even death with no inducement whatever except the hope of the fulfillment of the promises of Christ. And all of these promises look for a reward only after death, and the full realization of them would be an indefinitely long time after death when: "The Son of Man shall come in the majesty of His Father, accompanied by His Angels; and then He will repay each one according to his deeds." (Matt. 16:27).

These promises have no weight unless they are made by one who has the power to fulfill them. It is hard, however, to say which of the two primary teachings of Christ recorded in the New Testament received the greater stress: First, that He spoke as God and, Second, that the salvation He had come to win and to offer to all men was the all-sufficient incentive for Hope. In short, all Christ did was to ask for, and give evidence worthy of, supernatural Faith to be manifested in the form of supernatural Hope for a goal to be realized in terms of supernatural Charity having its fruition in eternity.

Here are some of His words: "Blessed are you when men revile you and persecute you. . . Be glad and rejoice because your reward will be abundant in heaven." (Matt. 5:11). "What would it profit a man if he were to gain the whole world, but forfeit his soul? " (Matt. 16:26). "Fear not little flock, for it has pleased your Father to give you the Kingdom. Sell your possessions and give alms; make yourselves purses which grow not old, an inexhaustible treasure in heaven." (Luke 12:33).

And St. Paul continually reiterates the same ideas: "For I hold that the sufferings of the present time bear no comparison to the glory that is to be revealed in us." (Rom. 8:18). "Eye hath not seen nor ear heard, nor has it entered into the heart of man to conceive what God has prepared for those that love Him." (I Cor. 2:9).

Obviously, if everyone took all this at its face value, no one would ever jeopardize his credit with God by any kind of sin. But why do we see so many who seem to act as if these things had never been said or as if they did not believe a word of it? The fearsome answer is that no one is compelled to believe or to hope and God has ordained that grace unheeded or spurned will be withdrawn so that blindness will not be healed.

That this is true was proved by some of those who were nearest to the most convincing evidence furnished by Christ Himself during the time that He dwelt among us. On the other hand, the early Christians, especially the Apostles and martyrs who *did* believe, have given us far more weighty evidence for the exercise of the virtue of Hope under conditions far more difficult than most of us will ever be called upon to test for ourselves.

When the Apostles were brought before the Jewish Sanhedrin after being jailed for their preaching, after cross-examination: "They flogged them and forbade them to speak in the Name of Jesus; then allowed them to go.

They therefore departed from the presence of the Council rejoicing that they were considered worthy to be treated with indignity for that Name." (Acts 5:40). Do we need a more urgent invitation than this for us to share with them the virtue of Hope?

St. Paul invites us in his letter to Titus thus: "For the grace of God has appeared to save all men, instructing us that, renouncing impiety and worldly lusts, we should live soberly, uprightly and religiously in the present world, awaiting the blessed hope and manifestation of the glory of our great God and Savior Jesus Christ." (2:11-14).

And St. Peter, in his first Epistle, repeats the invitation of St. Paul: "Blessed be God the Father of our Lord Jesus Christ! According to His great mercy He has begotten us again into a living hope, by the Resurrection of Jesus Christ from the dead; into an inheritance imperishable, unimpaired and unfading, reserved for you in heaven." (1:2-4).

How is it possible for us to be impervious to the urging of this evidence? I must admit that the study of the virtue of Hope involved in the preparation of this chapter has left me somewhat astonished at the mildness of my own enthusiasm in the past. It has given me far more active incentive to keep an eye on my conscience even as to the slightest sins that might mar that healthy longing for the fulfillment of my destiny which the virtue of Hope inspires.

I have said that the direct object of the supernatural virtue of Hope is God, but that only begins to tell the whole truth about this treasure. Just what do we mean by this statement? It means that Hope, inspired by Faith, is the incentive which causes us to conform our acts to the will of God as the means to bring us to that blessed state of union in love with God in the Beatific Vision in heaven. And just what does *that* mean? Again, we know by Faith that it means something different for every individual soul, depending on the degree of conformity to the will of God and cooperation with the grace of God in every act of a lifetime.

It is the sum-total, if that expression can be used in connection with something of infinite duration; it is the sum-total of our happiness derived from our individual capacity to enjoy the love of union with the infinitely perfect Being who has created this universe. He has created it in order to make us happy and, on the final Day of Judgment, He will restore all things to the perfect reflection of His own perfection with a new heaven and a new earth and new immortal bodies to be reunited with our souls for the most perfect enjoyment of it all.

What will it be like? We cannot know: not merely because we, in our finite nature, cannot imagine infinite perfection, but because our mortal state does not even provide the faculties to imagine with! "It cannot enter into the heart of man to conceive what God has prepared for those who love Him."

The nearest approach to comprehension possible for us is the realization that whatever our hope may inspire us to desire, the reality will be far better. We will enjoy all the love and companionship of our dear ones made perfect in mutual union with God. We will enjoy all the happy pursuits of this world made more intense by the perfection of our immortal faculties and the addition of other faculties and the renewed perfection of all created things.

One of my greatest joys in this world has been fly-fishing for steelhead with my wife. I will probably never wet a line again but I am confident that in the world to come some of the monsters I have failed to land will be waiting for me in still more perfect surroundings! All these things we will do, without interrupting the constant supreme happiness of doing it all, we might say, immersed in God's love which we can perceive in everything we do.

Now, we can only know this darkly with the knowledge of Faith. But Faith is aided by grace. If we use the grace of God to exercise the great virtue of Hope, we need no other monitor for our conscience in this world.

The Blessed Virgin Mary looking at the tiny helpless shivering Child lying in the straw of a manger, saw and adored God. The other inhabitants of Bethlehem saw only another destitute infant. The rich man "Dives" suffering in hell, begged Abraham to send Lazarus to warn his brothers to repent. And, though one who was God and Man rose from the dead to warn them, the many brothers of Dives will continue to resist the grace of God till the end of time.

Whenever I hear of the death of some blatant scorner of God, I often picture to myself the reaction of that soul as he is brought face-to-face with reality. Even, if by God's mercy, he is admitted to Purgatory, there is no word and no emotion adequate to picture his amazement at finding the truth compared with what his example has been.

In the words of our Savior which we sing in the liturgy of His Passion on Good Friday: "My people, what have I done to you? Or in what have I grieved you? Answer Me! What more should I have done that I have not done?" (The Reproaches).

Cannot we, with the eyes of Faith, see through the blindness of our human frailty and falling at the feet of the Risen Christ adore Him and beg His mercy as we sing in the closing verse of the "Te Deum": "Let Thy mercy O Lord be upon us; as we have hoped in Thee. In Thee, O Lord, have I hoped, let me not be confounded forever."

Study Questions:

1. Define the theological virtue of HOPE and explain the importance of its relationship to Faith and Charity.

2. What are the theological virtues; why are they so-called, and how do they "transmute every human act into the precious gold of eternal value?"

3. Discuss the "pay-day" of the virtue of Hope and relate it to the Bible story of Esau.

4. Elaborate the notion of supernatural merit as the coin which measures one's savings account in heaven and show the relationship of Hope in its earning.

5. Describe the kind of hope which opposes the supernatural virtue of Hope.

6. Discuss the natural virtue of hope giving an example of its functioning and compare it with the functioning of the supernatural virtue of Hope.

7. Elaborate the answer to the question: "Why is it, then, that anyone is ever slow to work at the supernatural virtue of HOPE?"

8. Quote from Scripture words of Christ and of Saint Paul which are invitations to the virtue of HOPE and show how they were unheeded even by some who were nearest to the evidence.

9. Elaborate the author's comment on his understanding of the virtue of Hope in preparing the material for this chapter.

10. Elaborate the answer to the question regarding heaven: "What will it be like?" and describe the reaction of the half-hearted who are granted admission to Purgatory.

CHAPTER IX
ABANDONMENT TO THE WILL OF GOD

Complete abandonment to God's will is the key without which very little of the precious treasures of true Christian living will come into our possession.

These treasures are spiritual and supernatural; namely, grace, merit and the pledge of far greater glory in heaven. We should now begin to realize that they are far more precious than any possessions which can be found in the world. In fact, they alone have true and lasting value.

As our appreciation of these treasures matures, we will welcome actual practical advice as to how to use the key to unlock the treasure-chest. Enough has been said to convince us that it is a very necessary part of our equipment for our life-work from this moment on, but not much has been said to teach us how to acquire it and put it to use.

The very first thing for us to do in our quest for this key to all virtue and goodness is to abandon all illusions as to its being something that can be acquired without effort on our part. This is true even though we know in theory that once gained it is easy to apply and when applied takes away all anxiety and frustration, all mental pain and fear. The reason that it is hard to gain and often requires a long struggle, is that it is directly opposed by self-love and pride: two of the characteristics of our fallen nature which are the most powerful tools of the Devil.

True humility, distrust of self and confidence in God are the three indispensable approaches to abandonment. Habitual pride gives little hope of cultivating humility. Wounded pride gives practically none at all. In like manner, thwarted self-love breeds malice rather than distrust of self; and stubborn clinging to the human will kills confidence in God.

These preliminary remarks are necessary by way of warning because abandonment to the will of God is not called for except when a situation arises where God's will as known is contrary to our natural human will. True, it may be said that we enter upon some project with "abandon" when it is something which we particularly enjoy doing. But in the sense which we are considering the word, it means to abandon some other course which we would otherwise take, in favor of a course which we believe conforms to the will of God.

This kind of abandonment may be considered under four different aspects: Positive and Negative; Active and Passive.

Positive abandonment is called for when our will has proposed a course which we already know or discover to be contrary to the will of God.

Negative abandonment is practiced in putting up with ourselves as God makes known to us our past sins, our imperfections, our faults, our weakness, our failures, out utter dependence upon Him. It also includes our whole-hearted approval of God's way of running the universe, which seems to be very different from what any human being would ever dream of!

Active abandonment calls for the conquest of self-love and the performance of God's will in spite of natural sloth, love of ease, and above all, in spite of human respect or human or material opposition and obstacles.

Passive abandonment covers perhaps the widest field of

all; acceptance of everything that happens to us, in peace and quiet and with resignation as being ordained by God.

Abandonment may be cultivated as to each of these four aspects separately. Practice in each contributes to the exercise of the others. All four must be achieved before self-mastery will replace self-love; distrust of self will take the place of pride; confidence in God will replace presumption and complacency in self. It must not be assumed, however, that these four aspects of abandonment are entirely distinct from each other. Each, in a sense, includes the others. Abandonment is one virtue, but it is perhaps easier to study and acquire it under these four headings.

As a foundation for the practice of abandonment, three ideas must be accepted and made an impregnable part of our mental frame-work:

The first applies to all four aspects of abandonment, but is perhaps most important as to the positive and active aspects. It is this: "Without Me you can do nothing." (Jn. 15:5). "With God all things are possible." (Matt. 19:26). No task, however formidable, need be feared if God furnishes the power. This applies particularly to our life-long combat with all sorts of temptation.

The second idea applies more directly to negative and passive abandonment and is this: Nothing whatever happens in the world without God's permission and in complete accordance with His plan. Nothing can happen which cannot be made beneficial to a soul really abandoned to God's will.

The third idea applies to all aspects and is this: Without the shadow of a doubt, God's will is made known to us by the infallible teaching of the Catholic Church and also the commands of those in authority over us.

The New Testament is replete with evidence that no spiritual profit is possible without uniting the human will with God's will, and its corollary that all things are possible when one collaborates with God. Outstanding among these is Christ's message to His Apostles at the Last Supper: "I am the Vine, you are the branches; if a man lives on in Me and I in him, then he will yield abundant fruit; separated from me you have no power to do anything." (John 15:5).

Nor was Christ exaggerating when the disciples, astounded at His warning that it would be easier for a camel to pass through the "Needle's Eye" than for a man who clings to riches to enter heaven, said: "Who, then, can be saved?" and Christ answered: "Such a thing is impossible to man's power, but to God all things are possible." (Matt. 19:26).

There is, however, no example of utter abandonment to the will of the Father in acknowledgement of His omnipotent power, equal to Christ's own in the Garden of Gethsemane: "And going forward a little, He fell upon the ground, and prayed: 'Father, all things are possible to Thee! Remove this cup from Me! Nevertheless, not what I will, but what Thou wilt.' " (Mark 14:36).

The measure of our faith is the measure of our ability to apply this principle of confidence in the power of God and to distrust self in favor of God's power. Christ said: "I promise you, if you have faith, though it be but as a grain of mustard seed, you have only to say to this mountain: 'Remove from this place to that!' – and it will remove; nothing will be impossible to you." (Matt. 17:20).

Here we have Christ's word for it that even a little faith can work miracles through the power of God. Cannot we, then, who have everything to gain and nothing to lose, muster enough faith to abandon ourselves all day long – in everything we do, to use this power of God? In other words, to bear fruit and to win treasure for ourselves and for others, through confidence in God alone and distrust of self!

The *second* principle requires no more faith to believe than does the first, but when it comes to actual appli-

cation in practice, it is tremendously difficult to pin it
right down and admit: "This means me." Let us restate
this principle in the first person singular: "Nothing has
ever happened to me without God's permission and in
accordance with His plan. Nothing *can* happen to me
which will injure me or which will not be a blessing to
me if I am really abandoned to God's will."

Perhaps the reader can never remember having been
tempted into grave sin. If so, you will not understand as
vividly as those who have, the force of this way of putting the matter. But even in your case, it applies to the
smallest sin as well — and you know what St. John said
about those who claim to have not sinned at all! (cf. I
John 1:10).

It is easy to see when we have resisted a temptation,
that it has been planned by God, and has given us profit.
But how about the case when we have failed and have
committed sin? It is most important to understand this!
God is never the cause of sin. In fact, He will always provide sufficient grace to enable every soul to resist every
temptation which He permits. As St. Paul tells us: "No
temptation has overtaken you but such as is incidental to
human nature, and God is faithful who will not permit
you to be tempted beyond your powers; on the contrary,
He will with temptation provide also the escape, so that
you may be able to bear it." (I Cor. 10:13).

God *does* permit temptation, and He will not deny our
free will to prevent us from committing sin. God permits
the sin to teach us our nothingness and to punish the
arrogance of our failure to distrust self and admit our
total need of grace.

If, however, you acknowledge the humiliation and
admit, with faith and love, the necessity of abandonment
to God; with confession and contrition and purpose of
amendment; God, who knows every thought, will cause it
to be a blessing to your soul, just as He did for Mary of

Magdala who became a saint from the depths of sin, through abandonment to God and distrust of self.

The same thing is true with reference to the trials of this life. God permits them and they cannot occur without His permission and in accordance with His plan. This is true of every trial, all the way from the little inconveniences of every day to the tragedies which may mark the turning point of lives. Every one, if accepted with the proper spirit of abandonment to God, can be a tremendous source of grace and merit. If we could only see how much grace and merit they may bring, we could more easily learn even to be grateful for them and never to complain of them.

As to the *third* principle, non-Catholics are obviously not prepared to accept as certain the proposition that the will of God is infallibly made known to us by the Teaching Authority of the Catholic Church. If they did, they could no longer remain non-Catholics. They will, however, perhaps agree that certain knowledge as to God's will, God's Revelation and God's law is more important than all other knowledge combined. It is, therefore, worth searching for more diligently than any other object in life. We Catholics should have it so firmly embedded in our understanding that no doubt can ever shake it loose.

We are all, however, so surrounded with the doctrines of atheism and materialism that we seem to find the very air we breathe contaminated with it. It is easy to absorb this contamination unconsciously without ever admitting any of the doctrine.

The materialist denies the spiritual and the supernatural. He therefore denies the sanction of God's commandments for the moral law. He is good only insofar as he thinks it will benefit himself. His criterion of action is present and future material comfort and freedom from pain — overlooking, of course, the pains of Hell. No sin is barred if it will bring him these ends without unpleasant complications.

And here is where the danger lies. He is so very numerous, and he is so blatant in defending his defiance of God's law, and generally he is outwardly so respectable, that we, while not admitting the soundness of his doctrine, will unconsciously, perhaps, take the attitude, "Everybody is doing it, including Catholics, and God is certainly not going to send everybody to Hell." "If I do what everybody else is doing, God will understand." Now, that may sound far-fetched to you; but I have heard Catholics use that very argument to justify sinful disregard of the observance of Sunday, and other sins of even greater malice. True, one's conscience will not let one commit grave sin without knowing it, but Satan can succeed with very clumsy tricks on people who *wish* to be deceived!

There are two points to be remembered here in keeping ourselves clean from contamination by the poison of the atheists and materialists, and in teaching others to do the same.

First: If one commits grave sin and does not repent; even if every other soul in the world is doing the same thing, God *will* send them all to Hell! Misery loves company, but company does not lessen the misery!

Second: The Church teaches some things that are not easy to obey except with the help of God's grace. The Church would change her teaching today and make it easier to be good Catholics, if God had not commanded her to teach all men His will, and made her to know what His will requires.

Furthermore, this law has been imposed by God on *all* men without exception. He has given them His infallible teaching Church, not only that they may know His law, but that through the Sacraments and the merits of Christ, they may be given the grace to make it easier to keep His commandments.

Never forget that refusal to believe does not free one from the law of God. Those who have rebelled have been allowed to become blinded as to the knowledge of the law, and have been deprived of the help of the Sacraments. We should never overlook the tragedy of this blinding, resulting from resistance to grace – and the preciousness of the treasure of grace in a soul.

God's law is not difficult for those who love Him and learn to abandon themselves to Him. Neither has God made His law hard just to plague us. His is a law of love. He only wants us to become perfect so as to be fit for Heaven.

The doctrines of materialism also affect the other part of this third principle and contaminate our loyalty to those whom God has placed over us in positions of authority. The tendency of this age has been to deny public authority and consider it "smart" to circumvent the officer of the law whom we ought to respect. But that is not what Christ taught. Christ even obeyed Pontius Pilate, reminding him that he would have no power or authority if it did not come from God.

And so it should be with every one of us. The institutions of our civil society and of our Church are governed by men and women who are human beings like the rest of us and subject to human frailty. But they have been placed where they are by God's permission. Even if we do not approve of their personal conduct, we cannot be abandoned to the will of God unless we are submissive to their authority.

This applies in the affairs of the world as well as in the affairs of the spirit. But for us who are seeking to learn how to gain the treasures of the spirit by abandonment to the will of God, it is a most important part of this third foundation principle.

Here and now, God's will is made known to us in various ways. Our spiritual and moral guidance comes to us through the Church. Our relations with other men and women are regulated by our various obligations: civil, family, and business; by law and by contract.

Parents in these days should be reminded of their responsibility before God to act as His instruments in behalf of their children. But the most important thing to remember is that every detail of the manifestation of God's will has come into being under God's supervision and in accordance with His complete control.

Every single officer who governs; every director who teaches, and you, dear reader, whether learning or teaching or otherwise ministering to others, have been prepared for this duty all of your life long up to this minute, by the loving Providence of God. In order to fulfill our duty and to show our gratitude for that Providence, each one should cooperate with all his heart for the benefit of all.

No better conclusion to these remarks of mine concerning the practice of abandonment could be devised, than the prayer with which St. Paul closed his Epistle to the Hebrews:

"Be obedient and subject to your prelates, for they watch over your souls as having to give account for them, so that they may do so with joy and not with sorrow; for this would by unprofitable for yourselves." ... "Now may the God of peace, who brought back from the dead the Great Shepherd of the sheep, our Lord Jesus Christ, with the Blood of an everlasting Covenant, make you perfect in all good for the accomplishment of His will, effecting in you what is pleasing in His sight through Jesus Christ, to whom be the glory throughout the ages of eternity. Amen." (Heb. 13:17 and 20-21).

Study Questions:

1. *Abandonment* is the "key" to the supernatural treasure chest; what are the treasures and what is the first warning as to the quest?

2. Name and briefly describe the four aspects of *Abandonment* then comment of their inter-relation.

3. Describe the three principles which form the necessary foundation for the *practice* of *Abandonment*.

4. Discuss the first of these principles, quoting three examples from Scripture.

5. Discuss the third principle for the practice of *Abandonment* with its reference to temptation and with reference to trials.

6. Discuss the third principle for the practice of *Abandonment* and give the suggestion for the consideration of non-Catholics and the danger of its contamination by atheism.

7. Elaborate the two points to be remembered for keeping clean from contamination by the poison offered by the atheists and materialists.

8. Discuss the extent of the binding force of God's laws and God's purpose in this binding men.

9. Name the various kinds of authority and discuss their status with respect to *Abandonment* and their defeat by atheism.

10. In conclusion, state God's part in all these considerations of *Abandonment*.

CHAPTER X

CHRIST'S SACRIFICE: THE CATHOLIC MASS

Perhaps the most important words ever spoken by a human being were the words of the God-Man who said: "Lo, I am with you all days even unto the consummation of the world."

The importance of these words derives from their context which clinches their meaning to be Christ's promise to remain as the invisible Head of His Church, protecting it from failure either temporal, spiritual or doctrinal.

There are, however, two other ways in which Christ's perpetual presence among us adds importance to these words. The fact of these two ways of being present is unknown to many non-Catholics; their sublime importance is too little appreciated by many Catholics. I refer, first, to the perpetual re-presentation of Christ's crowning act of atonement for sin by the shedding of His Blood upon the Cross, which is made present for us by the Sacrifice of Mass offered upon hundreds of thousands of altars around the world each day; second, to the personal Presence of Christ, remaining in the consecrated Host which by the all-but-unbelievable generosity of God, He has given to us as one of the fruits of His Sacrifice.

I will discuss these two precious gifts in this chapter and the next. The first of these gifts is the unbloody presentation of Christ's death upon the Cross, which we call the Sacrifice of Mass and which is the central and essential act of Catholic Christian worship.

It is difficult to know how best to approach this tremendous subject so as to give non-Catholics, in a few brief moments, a glimpse of its truth, and to try to awaken in Catholics a renewed appreciation of its preciousness. One feels a little of the bafflement expressed by St. John at the end of his Gospel when he said: "Were everything to be written down, not even the world itself, I imagine, would hold the volumes that should be written." (John 21:25). There has been more written and said about the Catholic Mass than one could read in a lifetime.

I have referred to it as "the all-but-unbelievable generosity of God." Probably the best way to begin is to amplify this idea. The generosity of God is so far beyond what any human being could possibly expect that the human mind rebels at belief when confronted by the truth at first glimpse.

This is magnified to the Nth degree when the matter presented for belief is a supernatural mystery which transcends the laws of natural science, and of which no man can fully explain the *"how"*.

The fact that the reality of Calvary is in the Sacrifice of the Mass is a pure mystery of Faith. It is stated, however, by Christ Himself with the words of consecration of the Chalice of wine which change it into His Blood on the altar by the supernatural process which we call transubstantiation. That is: the substance of the wine all becomes the substance of the Blood of Christ in the reality of His glorious Body and Blood, Soul and Divinity. "TAKE THIS ALL OF YOU AND DRINK FROM IT: THIS IS THE CUP OF MY BLOOD, THE BLOOD OF THE NEW AND EVERLASTING COVENANT. IT WILL BE SHED FOR YOU AND FOR ALL MEN SO THAT SINS MAY BE FORGIVEN. DO THIS IN MEMORY OF ME."

In like manner, the substance of the wheat bread is all transubstantiated into the Body of Christ, also in the reality of His glorious Body and Blood, Soul and Divinity.

"TAKE THIS ALL OF YOU AND EAT IT: THIS IS MY BODY WHICH WILL BE GIVEN UP FOR YOU." One receives *both* His Body and His Blood in *either* the Host or the Chalice. The substance is all changed into the substance of our God.

When Christ was preparing the Jewish people for this astounding piece of news, He said: "He who eats My flesh and drinks My blood, lives continually in Me and I in him." (Jn. 6:57). Whereupon many of His disciples refused to believe saying: "This is hard saying, who can be expected to believe it?" (Jn. 6:61). Instead of modifying this statement, however, as we have already seen, Jesus turned to His closest friends, the Apostles, and said to them: "Do you also wish to go away?" Simon Peter answered Him, "Lord, to whom should we go? Thy words are the words of eternal life; and we ourselves steadfastly believe and know that Thou art the Christ, the Son of God." (John 6:68-69).

That statement needs constant repetition by all of us today! The situation is not one whit different at the present time. No Catholic believes that a chemical analysis or any other scientific examination would disclose any difference between a consecrated Host and one not consecrated. But every Catholic knows that if he intentionally fed the first to a bird, he would be offering an insult to Christ and would be guilty of a sacrilege which, if not repented and confessed with true sorrow, would consign his soul to hell for all eternity.

Why does he know? For no other reason than that which made the Apostles know: because God said it was true and God has the power to make it true. The incentive to believe is no different today from what it was when the Apostles believed it from Christ. Modern scientific discoveries do not make it any harder to believe, nor do they make it any easier. The ordinary laws of physics have no bearing on the matter. How it was to be done, the Apostles had no idea, and we have no idea.

That it was to be done, the Apostles were to learn, and
we know it from them and would know it even if there
were no Bible. How could we possibly know it if there
were no Bible? I will tell you why — but that leads to
the explanation of the origin of the Catholic Mass.

It happened at the Last Supper, about a year later
than Peter's declaration of Faith that I have just
described. There Christ, on the eve of His Passion, consecrated the Apostles as His first priests and Bishops and
taught them how the triune God was to be worshipped
from then on until the end of time. He also gave them
the power to carry out His command. It was such an
unexpected way that no man living could possibly have
imagined it or invented it.

He told them that He was going to lay down His life
for the salvation of all who would unite themselves to His
will, just as He was uniting His will to the will of His
Father. He was doing this by submitting to His death
upon the Cross because it was the means of salvation for
men chosen by the Father. Therefore, it was for Him the
only suitable means.

He then told them that He wished them to continue
this Sacrifice of His Body and Blood which He was to
offer the next day, so that it would be present for all
men of all future time. Then, to their utter amazement,
He showed them how He intended to make this possible,
by the miracle of transubstantiation, which He had only
hinted at the year before when He had told them that He
was going to give them supernatural life by giving them
His flesh to eat and His Blood to drink.

For, as they were eating, Jesus took bread and blessed,
broke and gave it to His Apostles, and said: "Receive and
eat: This is My Body." And taking the Cup, He gave
thanks, and gave it to them saying: "Drink, all of you, of
this: For this is My Blood, that of the New Covenant,
which is poured out for you and for many for the remission of sins." (Matt. 26:26-28).

The very nature of the event makes it impossible that any man or group of men would have had the temerity to invent it or to try to report it falsely. That is why we know that it is true without reference to the Bible. This command of Christ was put into practice from the very first, long before any of the New Testament was written. Partly because of it, the Christians were subjected to persecution from the very beginning.

The fanatical Jewish leaders, like Saul of Tarsus, who became St. Paul after his conversion, were determined to stamp out the last vestiges of the power of Christ which seemed to them to oppose their temporal interests. And so the Christians were all facing torture and martyrdom from the beginning. They accepted death gladly rather than deny any of the doctrine or worship which Christ had taught them.

This first continuing of the offering of Christ's Sacrifice with His Body and Blood obtained in the manner and with the power bequeathed to them by Christ, gave their enemies an added handle to declare them worthy of death. They called them flesh-eaters and cannibals. Does it seem likely, under these circumstances, that one or more of them would have thought of inventing it when there had been eleven witnesses to the true event? If by some wild fancy they had invented it, would they have persevered unanimously under torture until death rather than admit the falsehood?

Most, if not all of the eleven original witnesses, as well as thousands of early converts were still living at the time this story was first put down in writing, ten to twenty years later, in the letters which began to accumulate to make up what became the Epistles of the New Testament. Does it seem likely that a falsification of the very essence of their worship would have been tolerated at that time?

No! If that had been the temper of their leaders, St. Paul would never have admonished the Galatians thus: "Even if we or an angel from heaven, preach to you, any

Gospel other than that which we preached to you, let him be anathema! " And then, in the vehemence of his fervor, St. Paul repeats: "As we have said before, so now I say again: If any one is preaching to you any other Gospel than that which you received, let him be anathema! " Then he continues: "Well, am I now trying to win men's favor, or God's? Or, am I seeking to please men? Were I still pleasing men, I should not be a servant of Christ's." (Gal. 1:8-10).

With the same intensity of expression, the same Paul said to the Corinthians: "For I received from the Lord what I delivered also to you, that the Lord Jesus, the night He was betrayed, took bread, and having given thanks, broke it, and said: "This is my Body which is for you: Do this in memory of Me." In like manner also the Cup, at the end of supper, saying: "This Cup is the New Covenant in My Blood: Do this as often as you drink it in memory of Me." For as often as you eat this Bread and drink this Cup, you proclaim the death of the Lord *until* He comes." (I Cor. 11:23-26).

St. Paul is here describing the essential action of the Catholic Mass, which makes present the death of the Lord today just as it did when St. Paul and St. Timothy celebrated Mass for the Corinthians, and just as it will be celebrated "until He comes" at the end of time.

This is the Sacrifice foretold by the Prophet Malachias who said: "For from the rising of the sun even to the going down of the same, My name is great among the Gentiles, and in every place there is a sacrifice, and there is offered to My Name a clean oblation: for My Name is great among the Gentiles, saith the Lord of Hosts." (Mal. 1:11).

Bear in mind, *we* are the Gentiles. It is *we* who offer this Sacrifice around the world which is most acceptable to the Lord God of Hosts. That is why the Catholic Mass is important. It is the prolongation of Christ's one infinite act of Redemption from which flows all worship, all

Faith, all Hope, all Love, all grace. It is Christ's act that makes it precious. All else is incidental. That is why one can participate in the Sacrifice of Mass with full benefit, even though he may not be able to hear the words that are spoken. The action is Christ's. The words are Christ's. He uses the hands and the voice and the person of an ordained priest as His instruments to repeat the same Sacrifice which He offered in His own hands at the Last Supper. This was the same Sacrifice which He consummated on the Cross on the following Day.

If this were all we could say of the Mass, it should make us eternally grateful and eternally eager to adore Him. But the *manner* of it — again, we must say, the all-but-unbelievable manner of it — makes those who understand it all-but-overwhelmed with wonder and amazement and love!

For, when Christ, using the hands and voice and person of His priest, performs the act of transubstantiation, just as He did at the Last Supper, and commanded His ministers to continue to the end of time, and says: "This is My Body", the appearance and the properties of the Bread in which it is performed remain the same, just as they did at the Last Supper. But by the power of God, the substance becomes His glorious Body and Blood, Soul and Divinity now reigning in heaven. And so God gives His glorious Self to us in a form which we can use as Food. In like manner He gives the same glorious Self in a form which we can use as Drink. In either one, in every particle or in every drop, He is whole and entire and glorious.

He gives us both so that by separation of Body and Blood we can offer the Sacramental Sign of the shedding of His Blood to the last drop in a clean oblation. And by the same divine power it becomes that Sacrifice in reality and truth. How does He do it? We do not know. Why does He do it, since we are so mildly grateful? It is hard to understand. *That* He does it, we have only His word. I submit that He has done enough to convince us that His word is Truth.

How far have we advanced along the road of our inquiry into Truth? We have seen that Almighty God created the world for man and made man in His own image; that is, with a spiritual soul and intelligence and free-will. Man abused these precious gifts by sin and made himself God's enemy. Instead of blotting man out of His creation, God with infinite generosity, left the splendor of His heavenly home and took upon Himself man's human nature. He did this for a twofold purpose inspired by love: *First*, because man could not be reinstated in God's favor by any act of his own. Only God could make an act of reparation adequate to atone for the offence against the infinity of God's offended dignity. *Second*: He came to teach all men what they need to know to enable them to share in this reinstatement and to avoid offending God again, and to provide the supernatural helps of grace without which man's spiritual life will wither and die.

His purpose was consummated on the Cross of Calvary when the God-Man sacrificed His life-blood to redeem mankind from the bondage of Satan. To make that too, present to all future generations He gave us the Ministering Church with the Holy Sacrifice of Mass and the seven Sacraments, which are so many channels of grace, deriving their efficacy from the same redemptive power of the God-Man's Sacrifice.

The greatest of all these Sacraments is the Body and Blood of the God-Man Himself, which, by the ingenuity of His love, He has contrived to give to us for physical and spiritual food, to unite us soul-to-soul with Himself as the crowning act of our participation with Him in the Sacrifice of Mass. And He remains with us as a perpetual Guardian and Friend all days even to the consummation of the world.

The Catholic Mass, as it is celebrated each day, all over the world by every priest, is not precisely the same as that celebrated by St. Peter and St. Paul in every detail. But it is precisely the same in its essence; namely, the fulfillment of Christ's command to: "Do this in commemoration of Me." That is, to re-present the Sacrifice of Calvary in a clean oblation from the rising of the sun until the going down of the same.

The worship of the Jewish Synagogue which was in part blended by the first Jewish converts into the Sacrifice of Mass, consisted in the reading of lessons from Scripture and the singing of psalms and canticles. And so the Teaching Church functions today with the preparatory prayers and lessons from the Bible, ending with the sermon and recitation of the Creed.

This part is sometimes called the Mass of Catechumens, the name applied to those receiving instructions, since in the early Church they were dismissed before the second part which contains the true Sacrifice and was secret in the early Church. Hence, the second part was called the "Mass of the Faithful." It is the essential part which Christ provides for all believing and baptized Christians to enjoy. This consists of the preparation of the elements for the Sacrifice, their consecration, the offering of the Sacrifice and the enjoyment of its fruits in Communion with the Body of Christ and thanksgiving for this mighty privilege.

There are, indeed, many Catholics who have grown up in the Faith who have left the Church because of some circumstance in their lives. They have turned away from this priceless privilege of reposing under the protection of God Himself and of being united with Him in Body and Soul. That tragedy could not happen to one whose faith has been really sure. No temporal reason could induce one to walk away from where he knows God is, to a place where God is not.

By the same token, one who is outside the Catholic Church, when he comes to understand the truth of the meaning of the Catholic Mass, if he believes in it, he could not possibly stay away.

Christ, our God, asks us to believe, but He will not violate our free-will. He stands at the door and knocks. "He who hears My voice and opens the door, I will come in to him and sup with him and he with Me." (Apoc. 3:20)

Study Questions:

1. State the words suggested as "perhaps the most important words ever spoken by a human being" and give three ways in which they have important meaning.

2. Comment on the "all-but-unbelievable" generosity of God in respect to these meanings.

3. Explain the meaning of the word "transubstantiation" and give approximately the words by which it is effected.

4. Compare the response of the Jews and of Peter to Christ's words with reference to giving them His flesh to eat, and discuss Peter's response as of today.

5. Describe the fulfillment of these words of Christ which came about in the following year and tell why we would know of it even if the Bible had not been written.

6. Emphasize the clinching of the authenticity of the Sacrifice of Mass by the martyrdom accepted by the believers who practiced it.

7. Discuss the clarification of the nature and purpose of the Mass put down many years later in the writings of the New Testament.

8. Elaborate the sentence: "It (the Catholic Mass) is the prolongation of Christ's one infinite act of Redemption from which flows all worship, all Faith, all Hope, all Love, all Grace."

9. What is the significance of the separate consecration of the Body and the Blood of Christ since He is wholly present in either?

10. Compare the Mass of today with the Mass celebrated by St. Peter and St. Paul and tell wherein they are identical, then comment on the state of mind of those who fall away.

CHAPTER XI

EMMANUEL

Up to now our attention has been directed quite largely toward the basic principles of the Catholic Religion; to explain what it is, how it came to be, and why Catholics believe that their salvation depends upon it. My object has been to present this subject for the information of the non-Catholic or the Catholic who needs help in understanding his Faith.

Now, if these basic things have been at least partly explained, it is time to have a heart-to-heart chat with the fervent Catholics who, by their lives and example, should be the ones who show forth the fruits of their Faith to the rest of the world. Non-Catholics can also learn much about what Catholics believe by listening to what they say to each other heart-to-heart.

We have talked about the central act of Catholic worship, the Catholic Mass. We have seen that it is a life-giving source of grace that flows out into the hearts of men and unites them to our Savior. It is the source of their salvation because it is the continuing presentation of the infinite Sacrifice of reparation made by Christ. It is applied to all who participate with Him in offering it to the Holy Trinity.

I have touched also upon that other fruit of the Mass, promised by Christ when He said: "Lo, I am with you all days, even until the consummation of the world"; that abiding presence of Christ upon our altars; that unexpected fulfillment of the prophecy of Isaias: "Behold a virgin shall conceive and bear a Son and His name shall be called Emmanuel." (Is. 7:14). It is this Emmanuel, which means God-with-us, that we Catholics should think of heart-to-heart today.

I have mentioned two things which seem to stand out above all others to make a Catholic different from everyone else in the world. Perhaps the most obvious one is that he believes that God is present in Person in the Catholic Churches throughout the world. The other stems from the same belief and is another way of clinching his certainty that Jesus Christ is true God and true Man. It is this; he honors the Blessed Virgin Mary as the "Mother of God."

Ever since the days when Jesus walked in person among the people of Palestine, there have been many who have found it difficult to believe that the Man, Jesus, had all the attributes of God; or, admitting that God has dwelt among us, that He had all the attributes of Man. "Is not He the son of a carpenter? Is not His mother called Mary, and His kinsmen, are they not all with us? " (Matt. 13:55). To honor Mary as the Mother of God makes it almost necessary to believe that the promises made by her Son with respect to His Church, were made by God and therefore could not have failed. To deny the visible continuity of Christ's Church, practically forces one to leave it somewhat vague as to just what is meant by the Divinity of Jesus of Nazareth.

Since Mary's claim to honor rests squarely upon her prerogatives as the Mother of God, the non-Catholic Christian cannot concede this honor without leaving unexplained his attitude toward the promises of her Son.

How much more directly, then, is it impossible for him to admit the Real Presence of God in the tabernacle on the Catholic altars. Certainly no man in his right mind would attempt to explain his membership in some other Church or in no church at all, if he admitted the belief that God Himself in Person is to be found in the Catholic Churches of the world, in the manner described by Himself at the Last Supper with His Apostles.

Every Catholic believes with all his heart that Christ is God, but how deep and intense and fervent is that belief? The same should be said one hundred times more earnestly with respect to the Real Presence of Christ in our churches. We fervent Catholics, of all people, should examine our consciences day by day to see how our thoughts and words and acts have tallied with the certain knowledge that God is always present in our church near by or under the same roof with us. He has imprisoned Himself here soley for the love of us to receive whatever love we may care to show Him. How hard it will be to reconcile some of our acts with that deep conviction of the proximity of Christ, which we can see even more vitally than we can perceive His presence indwelling in our souls.

When I was a fairly recent convert and a layman, the tremendous preciousness of this fact so impressed me that I wanted to try to do something to spread the consideration of it more widely among non-Catholics. So I wrote a little booklet entitled: "A Simple Explanation of the Catholic Mass for non-Catholic Visitors" – dedicated to "Our Lady, Help of Christians, who dearly loves to welcome visitors." I will quote a couple of paragraphs from that little booklet with reference to the Eucharist, which means "thanksgiving" but is also the name given to Christ present on the altar. It says:

> There is a part of the time during the Mass which you will probably recognize, when Christ Himself is actually present upon the altar. This is not something which Catholics have arrogated to themselves. We did not start it. We never would have dreamed of inventing it. It has been that way since Christ declared it to the world at the Last Supper. Even though you may find it impossible to believe this to be true, you will experience a very real spiritual benefit if you conduct yourself

in a manner suitable to the dignity and majesty of the presence of God.

In most Catholic churches there is a tiny house or tabernacle upon or near the altar and a light burns near it in the sanctuary. If you see this, you will observe that the people entering and leaving the church, genuflect before the tabernacle. This act of reverence is directed toward the tabernacle because the people believe that Christ, who is God, is actually present there, visible to our eyes only as the consecrated Host. They believe this because Christ said, "Behold, I am with you all days even unto the consummation of the world." and because He said in consecrating the first Bread, 'This is My Body.' You do not believe this or you would soon become a Catholic. You may reflect, however, that Christ said to St. Thomas, "Blessed are they who believe although they have not seen."

Most non-Catholics who realize this tremendous truth for the first time are deeply impressed. Whether they believe or not, they can understand why Catholics are so devout when attending Mass; why they make visits to the church when there is no service in progress, and why most of them are so zealous about their obligations to attend at Mass on Sundays and Holy Days.

But the thing that non-Catholics find hard to reconcile with this belief is the behavior of so many Catholics when they are away from Church. When non-Catholics begin to find out the truth about the Catholic Church, they begin to expect Catholics to have better morals than those who do not have that faith that God Himself is so close to them. They are scandalized when they do not find it. I know from experience in my younger days, and I was not looking for scandal either. When I began to find myself in love with a Catholic girl, it used to make me furious when the Catholic Church was put in a bad light in the newspapers by some scandal of morals. And then, I had not the faintest idea that I would ever be a Catholic.

Another thing that made me fairly sick at heart was a Catholic acquaintance who was most fervent about Mass and Communion every Sunday. But he sinned disgracefully every Saturday. To me it seemed as if he felt perfectly free to commit sin because he knew he could go to Confession the next morning. *Now*, I know that the young man simply did not know his Faith. But that man, and men like him, do untold harm to souls. Poor Mother Church is saddled with them and cannot cast them off while life lasts and there is a chance of their conversion.

But let me tell you, the same is true to the Nth degree when we faithful Catholics fail to give evidence of our appreciation of the presence of God among us. Catholics and non-Catholics alike, expect us to be good, charitable, gracious and kind for the love of God. Any evidence contrary to this expectation scandalizes them. I am using the word "scandalize" in its true sense which means: to lead into sin. This is so because it weakens the faith of Catholics, and defers the acceptance of the Faith by non-Catholics. I wish everyone could realize fully the evil and far-reaching effect of any of their words or acts which are not consistent with their certain knowledge of the Presence of God in the Eucharist. And this applied most of all in the heart of your own home! Fathers, Mothers, Children, Relatives — I beg you to listen and heed!

Please do not discount what I am saying. I know what I am saying and I know from experience that it is true. I do not mean to accuse you of malice in this regard, but I do mean that hardly one of us is entirely free from guilt.

To the extent that we could improve in the example of charity and awareness of God's presence, in every contact and conversation, above all, with our immediate family and associates, intimate and remote. To that extent we have not only an obligation stemming from our Faith, but also a priceless opportunity to make for ourselves a gold-mine of grace, virtue and merit, instead of a stupid waste of all the helps contained in the State of Sanctifying Grace which we have received at Baptism. In other words, instead of gathering the spiritual gold of happiness, we may be allowing ourselves to become buried in the worldly dross which separates us from God.

These· are somewhat harsh words and I do not like them in a talk about the precious Eucharist. But I beg every reader to make himself a committee-of-one to see that they do not have any application to him. If you will do that, then we can safely go on to enjoy the treasure which God has given to us in all its happy reality.

There is a special feast-day celebrated by the Church shortly after Pentecost each year. This Feast, called "Corpus Christi," does honor to this one item of God's goodness to men. The theme of all the prayers of the Church which are special for that feast-day, is the expression of gratitude and worship of the God-Man present before our eyes in the consecrated Host.

St. Thomas Aquinas, who died almost seven hundred years ago and who is called the Angelic Doctor, partly because of his devotion to this presence of Christ, is the author of several of the beautiful prayers and hymns used on this day. The hymn composed by St. Thomas for the office of Lauds on the Feast of Corpus Christi, contains four lines which inspired a king of France to say: "I would give my realm to have had the grace to be the author of those words." The verse, approximately translated from the Latin, is this:

> *Se nascens dedit Socium*
> *Convescens in edulium*
> *Se moriens in Pretium*
> *Se regnans dat in Praemium*

> Himself, aborning He gave as Friend
> Himself, while dining, He gave as Food
> Himself, in dying, He gave as Ransom
> Himself, God reigning, He gives as Victory.

Each of these lines should make us shout with joy. Each is a sufficient invitation to the Catholic Faith. Each is a revelation of a mystery of God's goodness.

As Friend in the tabernacle, He is one Person we can always count on. He will never fail us. Not only will He never fail us, but He will give the perfect solution of every problem of our life, *provided* we go to Him with perfect abandonment to His will, prepared to listen humbly as well as to tell Him our needs.

The more time we spend with this Friend in the tabernacle, the more certain it becomes that no cloud will ever darken our joy, and the more evident it becomes that we are on the road to sainthood. One cannot contemplate the goodness of this Friend day by day, and at the same time fail to be united with His will.

It is significant that our Lord gave us this great and precious mystery of our Catholic life while celebrating a festive banquet with His closest friends. Christ seemed to want to emphasize that while all else was tragically sad, this part of the events of His Passion should be a joyous one. While His loved ones would later learn to cherish the Eucharist because of His abiding presence, they would first receive it as part of the food and drink of a banquet.

Now, food has four quite separate functions: To nourish, to repair, to promote growth and to give delight. How perfectly our Lord fulfills these functions with the precious Food of His love. Just as the body is nourished, day by day, with the food we receive, so does He nourish the soul with the daily "supersubstantial" Bread of His Body. Just as proper diet restores and repairs the healthy functioning of our organic life, so is the health of Sanctifying Grace kept in repair by the tonic food of daily Communion with Christ.

St. John, in the opening words of his Gospel, gives us these words of rejoicing: "But as many as received Him, to them He gave the power to become the sons of God." That is, we who have received the precious Eucharist, have been *born* into the household of God to *grow up* into saints, fed by this heavenly food. God has repeatedly shown us that our spiritual growth accomplished by the Eucharist, is the real purpose of our sojourn in this world.

The delight which we derive from the privilege of

Communion is only limited by the obscurity of our Faith. We know that its consummation in the Beatific Vision, which is the vision of God in heaven, is the purpose of our creation. Christ will give us a fore-taste of that delight to the extent that we unite ourselves, soul to soul, with His presence in our Holy Communion.

St. Thomas' line: "*Se moriens in pretium* – Himself, in dying, He gave as Ransom" – should fill our hearts with gratitude each time we participate at the Holy Sacrifice of Mass and whenever we receive Communion. This central act of Christian worship is the perennial extension of the ransom of our souls by means of the infinite satisfaction of Christ's bloody sacrifice in our behalf.

We will never exhaust our obligation to adore, not only the fact, but also the manner of our Redemption which is re-enacted for us every day upon the altar. That is why people of every age and degree of understanding can participate with equal benefit in the Sacrifice of Mass. Once one understands that the Mass is a re-enactment for us of the drama of Christ's Sacrifice, in which His infinite wisdom and mercy have combined all of those blessings immortalized by those four lines of St. Thomas, his participation may be complete.

For, in the very words of consecration of the Host, it is as if He were born anew for us to remain with us as our most staunch and loving Friend. And to make it doubly precious, He has effected it in such a beautiful way that His Sacred Body is to become our Food and so make for us a sensible means of physical union, not only with Him, but through Him, with all the other souls united with Him all over the world and in Heaven, but especially with those who receive together with us.

Then, by the separate consecration of the Chalice of His Blood, there is created the Sacramental Sign of the shedding of His Blood to the last drop, on the Cross as a *Ransom* "for you and for many for the remission of sins." Since sacramental signs cause what they signify, there *is* then, the Sacrifice of Calvary re-presented before us so that we have the privilege of immediately sharing with Him the *Victory* over death which He so graciously won for us.

And by this subtle benevolence of God's love, all this is accomplished for us in the Substance of His glorious Body and Blood, Soul and Divinity, now reigning in Heaven. Only God could plan such perfect harmony of treasure. Only God could make it true!

There are many ways of assisting at Holy Mass. For those who attend regularly and frequently, there is no better way and no more fruitful way than to participate, word by word and act by act, with Christ who is using the voice and hands of the priest as His instruments on the altar. But however you may be able to join in the action, never forget that Christ is bringing this action before you here and now, so that you too may learn to *live* the Sacrifice of Mass in your own life by sharing with Him your love, time and energy in the service of God and your neighbor.

When you thus manifest the love which should be the power that sustains your whole life, then, by your generous sacrifice, you are "filling up what is lacking in the suffering of Christ." Then, you will be rewarded one hundred-fold by sharing also with Him the Victory.

"Put on, therefore, as chosen ones of God, holy and beloved, a heart of compassion, kindliness, humility, mildness, long-suffering. Bear with one another and forgive one another, if any one has a complaint against anybody; just as the Lord forgave you, so you also should do. And over all these put on love, which is the bond of perfection. And let the peace of Christ, to which also you were called in one body, be supreme controller in your hearts. And be grateful! " (Col. 3:12-15).

Study Questions:

1. Characterize the preceding chapters and state the perspective for discussing *Emmanuel* = God with Us.

2. Recap the non-Catholic view of the two natures in Christ; Mary the Mother of God; and the Real Presence of Christ in the Tabernacle.

3. Mention the "examination of conscience" needed to reconcile our behavior with our belief in the proximity of the Presence of Christ.

4. Summarize the paragraphs quoted from the author's Simple Explanation of the Catholic Mass for Non-Catholic Visitors and comment on the reaction of non-Catholics.

5. Describe the author's distress as a non-Catholic, when comparing belief in the near presence of God with the scandalous behavior of some Catholics.

6. Elaborate the following sentence taken from context: "I wish everyone could realize fully the evil and far-reaching effect of any of their words or acts which are not consistent with their certain knowledge of the presence of God in the Eucharist."

7. Quote (approximately) and comment on St. Thomas' hymn for the Feast of Corpus Christi.

8. Comment on Christ's intention in the institution of the Eucharist at a banquet.

9. Comment on the sentence: "We will never exhaust our obligation to adore, not only the fact but also the manner of our Redemption which is re-enacted for us every day upon the altar". and relate it to St. Thomas' hymn.

10. Elaborate the sentence: "There are many ways of assisting at Holy Mass."

CHAPTER XII

PRAYER: THE ACME OF ABANDONMENT

The most effective positive approach to the practice of abandonment to the will of God is prayer; the most effective obstacle is sin. This should give us an incentive to make all our action into prayer and a potent reason for hating sin. But while we are learning, there are some things that need a place in our kit of tools for the work in hand.

The first is a sound respect for the value of every minute of every hour of every day, not only on Sunday, but every day of the life of each one of us.

Abandonment of God's will can become automatic if one cultivates the habit of being constantly and actively aware of His presence and the treasure of His partnership.

Prayer, any prayer, is an expression of a desire for perfection and an act of conformity to the will of God. For who would be so unperceiving as to pray without the intention of becoming better; and who would presume to address God without the intention of being submissive to His will. True, there are mercenary souls who do not scruple to ask favors from God with little or no love for Him, unless He earns it by conforming to their will. There are also Pharisees today who like to stand and compliment themselves in God's hearing. But such approaches to God are not prayers and to call them such is to add insult to injury against God's goodness and mercy!

How far they fall short of the title of prayer can

readily be seen when we examine Father Tanquerey's definition of prayer. He defines true prayer as: "An elevation of our soul to God to offer Him our homage and ask for favors in order to grow in holiness and for His glory." If we can fulfill that definition in our prayers, we are already miles ahead in our pursuit of perfection! Let us study it to see why.

The very first phrase, "elevation of the soul to God," carries with it the idea of detachment from creatures and even from self-love, in order to take full advantage of that intimacy of God's presence by devoting our attention exclusively to Him. The more we learn to exercise this advertence to God's intimate presence, the more precious it will become to us and, most important of all, the more we will be able to extend the spirit of prayer into everything we do. Even our worldly pursuits which demand concentrated attention will be enriched by this spirit of prayer.

When someone we love is in the room where we are working or studying or reading, there is an atmosphere of communion of intention even though never a word is spoken directly. But, in order for that loving communion to exist, it must have been established by direct communication of thoughts and acts of love. And so it is, in still higher degree, in our loving relationship with God. He is always present to us, always loving us, always ever dwelling in our souls unless we have deliberately closed our hearts by grave sin. But our love for Him is measured by our degree of advertence to His presence. It is built upon this loving elevation of the soul to Him, always there, always ready to receive us and reward us with graces of increased faith and hope and love.

There are various ways to practice this continuous elevation of the soul to God after direct and formal prayer. The commonest and easiest way is to cultivate the habit of ejaculatory prayer which can be carried on at the core of one's soul even while doing other things. I have had people tell me that they would feel utterly embarrassed and insincere and hyprocritical as well as disedified if they were asked to make the ejaculation: "Jesus I love you", over and over again. I can sympathize with them because I have had the same feeling myself. But I can also assure them from experience that, with practice, all that feeling of repugnance will disappear and it will not only be sincere but it will be immensely helpful for their spiritual development. Jesus will see to that!

In fact, it is safe to say that perfection cannot be successfully pursued without some such habitual attitude of prayer. If the expression: "Jesus, I love you" sounds over sentimental to you, any simple expression will do. There is no better ejaculation than the phrase of the Lord's Prayer, "Thy will be done" or the single Latin word "Fiat" which means the same thing: "Fiat voluntas Tua." I can assure you that if you will begin this easy practice and keep it up, it will be the most useful thing you have learned thus far in your pursuit of perfection.

And here is another most important point to keep in mind; prayer, whether it be worship or petition, is not a unilateral performance but, to be effective, it must be a conversation or, in the language of theology, a "colloquy." In other words, it involves listening as well as speaking to God.

Now, to open any kind of conversation with almighty God our first act should be one of homage. When we meet a friend on equal terms, we do not begin a conversation, especially one of petition, without a salutation giving honor suitable to his dignity. How much more is due to God who is the Author of our very life and hence our infinite Benefactor. We, therefore, elevate our souls to God, according to our definition, to "offer Him our homage and ask His favors."

That word "favors" introduces a new thought which it is important to understand at the very beginning of our pursuit of perfection. It is no sin, and may be a very pure form of submissive prayer, to ask God for material and temporal favors such as a raise in pay or a happy marriage or sunshine or rain, *but* only with the proviso that our estimation of our temporal needs is utterly subject to the wisdom of God, and that our confidence in Him and our love for Him are detached entirely from His answer to such a prayer.

That is why Father Tanquerey's definition of prayer immediately specifies the reason for the favors requested as: "in order to grow in holiness for His glory." Now, you may very well ask: "Is it really honest to ask for nothing but holiness for God's glory, when what I really want is decent weather for my party?" And that emphasizes the point which I have just tried to make. We must never pass judgment upon God's management of our temporal affairs other than to say: "Thy will be done."

It is perhaps hard for most of us to believe honestly that even our own sanctification has for its principal motive the glory of God. But let us try to accept it on faith that giving glory and gratitude to God will be the principal item of our joy and beatitude in heaven. It will make everything else that we hope to do there have meaning and satisfaction. To the extent that we are able to let this idea sink into our immortal souls here and now, to that extent we will find true prayer easy and natural.

All prayer has a two-fold end — to worship and to beg. The purest prayer of all is adoration of God for what He is. Rightly conceived, it springs from pure Charity and includes within itself utter joy of thanks for our awareness through faith and contrition for the inadequacy of our response to this awareness. We adore and say: "Oh Lord, I believe. Help Thou my unbelief!" — and the words of the Gloria: "We praise Thee, we bless Thee, we adore Thee, we glorify Thee, we give thanks to Thee for Thy great glory, Lord God, heavenly King, God the Father almighty!"

Thus far, I have been discussing individual private prayer in general. I have hinted that it can become a continuous and habitual awareness of the presence of God in the soul. In order to bring that about, however, one must devote some time each day when awareness of the presence of God is the principal business in hand. In other words, one who seeks to have God for a Partner must learn to *practice* mental prayer.

In the school-rooms of our childhood we used to see mottoes hanging on the wall to remind us constantly of some of the essential habits for successful life. Here is a motto which I wish you would write on the front page of your memory: "For healthy Christian life, there is no substitute for daily, one might almost say hourly, individual conversation with God in mental prayer." There is no active apostolate, no heroism of religious endeavor, not even the heroism of martyrdom that can be expected to take the place of that constant companionship with God which is generated and acquired in the time we spend in quiet meditation on the goodness of God and the gratitude we owe to His divine majesty. And please do not set this idea aside with the thought that I have become used to talking with Religious. It applies equally to every Christian!

Just what, then, is mental prayer? First, let me make one thing clear — the adjective "mental" used to describe prayer never needs to mean that it is prayer without the use of words. It merely means that word concepts of the mind need not be made vocal or articulated by the lips, although they may be, without destroying the quality of mental prayer. The only essential quality which distinguishes mental prayer is that it is an individual and personal mental contact or union with God in any form that may suffice to maintain that contact.

It is always a supernatural elevation of the mind and heart to God in acts of love or praise or worship or thanksgiving or petition, with or without mental or vocal words. But please know this from the very beginning: every Christian in a state of grace is capable of mental prayer. Indeed one cannot remain in a healthy state of grace without a reasonable amount of this nourishment of mental prayer. The point I want to make clear is that mental prayer is the ordinary way of maintaining spiritual health, and is not a special privilege that comes only after years of apprenticeship in some inferior form of prayer.

Of course, there are exalted states of mental prayer which are special gifts to a chosen few. But, so precious is the ordinary gift of mental prayer which may be said to be freely available to all who will make a real honest effort, that it is nonsense to remain aloof from it because the apex seems remote. It is like saying that no one should seek to enjoy the pleasures of singing because the chances of reaching grand opera are too remote.

This comparison, however, is inadequate for two reasons. *First:* mental prayer is a supernatural act and so requires grace which makes it meritorious in any degree of proficiency. *Second:* it is inadequate chiefly because the preciousness of any degree of ability to exercise affective acts of prayer is more to be desired than the most exalted success in any other pursuit of this life! And that is not an exaggeration!

The use of a book of so-called "meditations" during the time set aside for mental prayer, no matter how holy and spiritual the book may be, is only a help to mental prayer. The time spent reading it is used in giving consideration to the ideas of someone else in the hope that it will stimulate ideas within us that will enable us to approach close to Christ in intimate conversation, as one would converse with a friend whom one loves with a love which exceeds any other earthly love. In addition, it is heightened by the awesome thought that *this* Friend is the God who is responsible for everything we have to be grateful for. This is the atmosphere of mental prayer. The time spent in reading may produce this atmosphere but it cannot be said to *be* the atmosphere.

Affective mental prayer of this kind stems from the will and intellect. It should not be confused with the word *affection*, which is ordinarily associated with the sense emotions. The most sincere, perhaps the most *effective* form of *affective* prayer can, and perhaps should be devoid of any sensible emotion of fervor.

Spiritual union with Christ is brought about in that part of the soul which is farthest removed from the material reactions of sense, but this does not mean that it cannot be on the same intimate terms as conversation with a friend whose presence one can reach out and touch. In fact, the spiritual conversation with Christ is more intimate than one with any other friend could be, because, on Christ's side, all that you can *think* is known as well as all that you mentally say.

That is one reason why mental prayer is so conducive to holiness. We cannot deceive even ourselves that our expression of love is sincere when all the time our conscience is shouting over our shoulder telling Christ in our hearing that our previous actions or thoughts give the lie to what we are trying to express in mental words. The result is that we humbly straighten the matter out and admit our fault with contrition or we stop praying.

That interference of conscience brings us to another and perhaps, for most of us, the main difficulty of maintaining intimate loving conversation with Christ for any length of time without the help of a crutch in the form of a book. It is the interference of distractions. These stem from very many sources, but the chief sources of distractions are self-love and obscurity of faith.

The command: "Thou shalt love the Lord thy God with thy whole heart and thy whole soul and thy whole mind and thy whole strength, and thy neighbour as thyself for the love of God," is definitely modified as to self-love by that last phrase: "for the love of God." The love which we bestow upon ourselves and our neighbor which stems from the love of God is very, very different from the self-love that brings about distractions in prayer. In fact, the latter is not entitled to the dignity of the name of love, since it is second only to actual sin in preventing our abandonment to the will of God.

So let us consider more carefully this annoying human failing of distractions in prayer. Probably no one that ever lived has been entirely free from this blight on the perfection of prayer. We are like the little boy who had been pestering his father for a pony. Finally, the father agreed to provide a pony if the boy would recite one "Hail, Mary" without any distractions. Immediately the boy dropped to his knees and said: "Hail Mary, full of grace, the Lord is with thee; Father will it have a saddle and bridle?" How easy it is to spoil our prayer by always dragging in ourselves and our petty self-love!

Our first attack against distractions then, must be to try to find a remedy for the principal causes, self-love and weak faith, which work together against us. If our faith could only bring to our souls the reality of Christ's presence as it actually is before us when we pray; if we could only see the love that His glorious but invisible face showers upon us; if we could only know the individual attention that Christ's omnipotence enables Him to bestow upon each one of us; our self-love would melt like wax into humble devotion before the furnace of His charity, as if for each one of us alone.

I say: "If we could." Well, we are not entirely helpless in that regard. True, faith is a gift from God, but it is also an act of the will. So, as St. Paul tells us, we can stir up faith from both of these sources. We can constantly remind ourselves of the intimate presence of God, especially when we pray. We can make wordless acts of faith, either in His glorious presence, or in His presence looking down on us from the Cross. We can also pray with the father of the boy who was possessed: "O Lord, I believe, help Thou my unbelief."

These spiritual aids against distractions can also be supported by natural means. The science of Psychology tells us that attention, which is the opposite of distraction, is an act of the will. Furthermore, acts of the will are determined by a combination of the influence of knowledge and motive. Therefore, the best strategy in opposition to distractions from adoration of the unseen presence of God, is the cultivation of knowledge and motive which His glory will shed upon the eyes of our mind.

This fact of science was crushingly illustrated for a friend of mine not long ago when, as a loving father, he burst into the dining room to give his tiny daughter a good-morning kiss, just as the door swung open from the kitchen and mother entered with a tray. As he leaned over to enjoy the usual glad response of the little one, he was considerably taken aback when a tiny palm kept him at arm's length while the happy smile was directed, not in his direction, but toward the tray, and his smiling greeting was repulsed by the calm but decisive ejaculation: "Bacon coming! " — Real devoted attention to one thing usually involves withdrawal from everything else.

To proceed, then, in our practical campaign against distractions, we must realize that, for the most part, they are merely the output of habits which form the pattern of our daily lives. The proper ordering of these habits can minimize the occurrence of distractions at their source and that can be a life-work for each of us all day every day.

First, there is carelessness and lack of reverence about our manner of prayer and our participation in liturgical action of every kind; thoughtless use of the sacramentals such as holy-water, the sign of the Cross, bowing at the Name of Jesus, irreverent posture, continual fidgeting, outward want of decorum. When we allow the body this lack of mortification, we cannot expect that the spirit will be free from a share in it.

Second, and very potent among habitual faults which court distractions, is carelessness about small sins. No one who is honest in his quest for perfection can tolerate that detestable alibi: "Oh, it's only a venial sin." Not only does such an attitude court every type of distraction, but it does so because it puts a thick lukewarmness between the will and the indwelling presence of God residing in the innermost depth of the soul. It thereby closes the door which leads to the way of perfection. No one can hope to make progress against distractions until he has cleared the atmosphere in his spirit between himself and the Heart of Christ. Venial sin and lukewarmness are the twin blunters of grace which elicited from Christ the ominous reproof: "I would that thou wert cold or hot. So, because thou art lukewarm and neither hot nor cold I am about to vomit thee out of My mouth." (Apoc. 3:16). What a pitiful plight it is to be so near and yet so far from the power of God's grace!

Another full-time propagator of distractions is curiosity, and especially the insatiable quest for news. In school or cloister we call one so addicted a "grapevine sleuth." Such thirst for the details of our neighbor's sayings and doings or an inordinant penchant for receiving letters; all these must be paid for by those inexorable distractions. Wasted hours before the T.V. screen cater fatally to the fault of curiosity.

A fourth prodigal source of distractions is one which perhaps lends itself most readily to discipline. It is want of custody of the senses. We have all been taught from childhood to turn away from that which is immodest or improper in speech or otherwise offers temptation to sin. So with every one of the senses – making little sacrifices for the sake of discipline is the very best way to strengthen the will in overcoming all the faults on the payroll of that gangster who rules distractions.

But as I have said earlier in this chapter, the habit of ejaculatory prayer is the ever-present and most potent moderator of distractions. Its neglect will court defeat. There is never a time when ejaculatory prayer is inopportune. There is never a time when it will fail to be useful in bringing us close to the greatest of all killers of distraction — attention to the indwelling presence of Christ!

There is one last word about prayer that we know from God Himself — public prayer is more efficacious than any private prayer. Participation in the Sacrifice of Mass is the supremely efficacious act of public prayer.

Study Questions:

1. Give Father Tanquery's definition of *prayer* and comment on it.
2. Compare our silent response to the presence of one we love with our loving relationship with God and state what causes each to exist.
3. Give the author's comment about the habit of ejaculatory prayer.
4. What is the meaning of the word *colloquy* applied to prayer?
5. Comment on the clause in the definition of prayer: "and ask Him favors" and tell how it is modified by what follows.
6. Describe what is called "the purest prayer of all."
7. Give a summary of the author's comment on mental prayer.
8. Comment on the use of a book of "meditations" during the time set aside for mental prayer, emphasizing the intimacy of the relationship involved in mental prayer.
9. Discuss the problem of distractions in prayer and comment on the two principal causes, self-love and weak faith.
10. In the campaign against distractions there are four habits of life which need proper ordering to minimize their occurrence. Name and discuss them.

CHAPTER XIII

CHRIST: OUR MODEL

Christ's Sermon on the Mount, which comprises the fifth, sixth and seventh chapters of the Gospel of St. Matthew contains the following passage:

> But I tell you, love your enemies, bless those who curse you, do good to those who hate you, and pray for those who revile you and for those who persecute you: so that you may be children of your Father who is in heaven, who causes his sun to rise upon the good and the bad, and rains upon the just and the unjust. . . . Do you therefore be perfect as your Heavenly Father is perfect. (Matt. 5:44-48).

These words of our Lord Jesus Christ when read carefully and thoughtfully, are almost certain to give the ordinary human being a definite shock of surprise. Even those of us who have a definite urge to abandon ourselves to the will of God, find that these admonitions are so far from the natural inclination of the will that we begin to wonder how literally and how imperatively Christ intended them to be taken.

In fact, when we find the admonition to love our enemies compared to God's generosity in sending rain and sun to benefit the unjust, we are inclined to regard them as generalities of variable application.

This conclusion, however, is, or should be, shattered when we come to the end of the passage and find that our Lord admits of no compromise. In fact, He goes beyond all human limitations, and commands us to be perfect — not just humanly perfect, but divinely perfect, as is God the Father in Heaven.

The shock of this realization may cause us to re-read with the same careful attention all of the admonitions found in the rest of the Sermon on the Mount.

We find that He begins by naming eight very unexpected routes to salvation. Unexpected, that is, to the Jews who heard them for the first time, and also unexpected to us when we detach ourselves from the Christian atmosphere in which we may have lived, and consider them only in the light of the tendencies derived from our fallen human nature.

Let us look at them: Poverty of Spirit: This rightly taken means recognition of our own nothingness, our utter dependence upon divine help. As St. Francis de Sales beautifully expresses it: "We are beggars in spirit."

Meekness: This is really an extension of poverty of spirit. It combines the virtues of temperance, patience, fortitude and charity toward our neighbor, solely for the love of God.

Acceptance of Bereavement: Those who mourn with resignation to the will of God are sure to find comfort in His all-embracing love.

To Hunger and Thirst after Righteousness: This is to seek with all one's heart to know and do the will of God.

To Show Mercy: This is not a natural tendency except when it stems from the recognition of God's love for our neighbor.

Purity of Heart: This is the characteristic of union with God in abhorrence of all deliberate sin and cooperation of the will with the grace of God.

Peace-Makers: These are the ones who, combining all these virtues, set aside their own immediate advantage and become reconciled even to injustice in order to promote God's glory and follow His will.

But perhaps the most difficult of all is to seek to do the will of God even when persecuted for our efforts.

Here the Catholic must face the facts. The very reason why his practice of religion has been so hated and persecuted is that it is so contrary to the natural, unbridled tendency of human nature. Every departure from the rule of life taught us by Christ proposes some easier course, or denies the possibility of carrying out all the demands of Christ contained in the Deposit of Faith which He has sent down to us from the Apostles.

And so a new idea begins to dawn upon the Catholic and also the Non-Catholic who has convinced himself that the only safe road to salvation is to "hunger and thirst" to know the will of God and to conform to His will when known — *cost what it may*!

The new idea is this: The commands of Christ seem to be quite difficult of acceptance by the natural human will. Yet Jesus Christ, true God and true Man, showed us in the life of His humanity that they can all be fulfilled perfectly by a human being. Surely then, this ineffable plan of our Salvation and Redemption by means of the Incarnation must have been intended to show us that Christ's admonition to man to be "perfect-as-God-is-perfect," can be fulfilled by man if he takes for his Model the God who became Man.

The more one ponders this idea, the more tremendous it becomes. Even though, at first glance, one may not quite understand why God sets such store by these difficult and mortifying virtues, it becomes easy to see that He has a perfect *right* to do so when we observe that God Himself was willing to give us the example of perfection in the practice of them.

Furthermore, for God, whose glory and majesty we can only faintly guess, to submit Himself to persecution and torture by the creatures whom He has made, is an infinitely greater exhibition of these virtues than would be possible for man.

Not only did Christ make Himself obedient to His own creatures, but, as St. Paul so vividly expresses it:

"Being minded as was Christ Jesus: Though he was divine by nature, he did not consider his being on an equality with God a thing to be grasped: but on the contrary, he emptied Himself, took the nature of a slave, and was made like to men. Then, having come in human form, He humbled himself, becoming obedient unto death — even the death of the cross! " (Phil. 2:5-8).

Christ gave us this example of heroic virtue, first and foremost because, as He constantly told us: "I seek not My own will, but the will of Him who sent Me." (John 5:30). If Christ, who is our God, went to such lengths of suffering to do the will of His Father, how much more should we be willing to do whatever He asks of us!

For God, the Creator of the universe, to become man at all, is a greater exhibition of humility than would be possible to man. Yet, not only did He become Man, but He became the most perfect example of humility among men.

It is this truly amazing feature of Christ's ministry upon earth which has been a stumbling-block for the worldly-minded in all ages. It is especially evident today in the attitude of those who hold up the so-called backward character of many predominantly Catholic nations as evidence of the inadequacy of the Deposit of Faith for the modern age. They compare it with what they call the "progress" of the nations which they describe as being emancipated from the domination of Christ's Vicar upon earth.

Yes, man is always prone to ask: "Why did the merciful God ask His Son to undergo such depths of suffering in His Passion? " The only answer Christ gave us was that it was to do the will of the Father. So, while we will never fully understand the reason for suffering as long as we remain in this world, we know that the superabundant suffering of Christ had a two-fold purpose:

First: to show God's hatred of sin; to show man the

infinite malice and hatred toward God involved in man's refusal to seek to do the will of God whose infinite love is responsible for man's existence from moment to moment. To impress indelibly on man's mind that not only is his sin so evil that only God-made-Man could offer adequate reparation to the offended Godhead, but that the magnitude of the evil is such that the God-Man whose least act of reparation has infinite value, found it "necessary" as He said, to go to the limit of human capacity in submitting His Humanity to torture to the last drop of His Blood upon the Cross!

Second: To show the infinite extent of God's love for those who would turn away from their sin and detest it and cleave to the will of God. For any man to lay down his life for another is, as Christ has told us, evidence of love which cannot be excelled. For God Himself to do so for His creatures is such superabundant evidence of infinite love that it has been disbelieved all down the centuries by those who refuse to respond to Christ's love by placing their wills at His disposal, repenting and confessing their sins.

But for those who do believe, it is a compelling motive to make them wish to kneel at the feet of Christ who has made Himself their Brother and to beg Him to be their Model in everything they do; to enable them to exercise this power to become the sons of God which He has won for them.

If we are moved by this compelling motive to take Christ for our Model, what is the first thing we should observe that is to be copied? Christ Himself has made that abundantly clear. Nine hundred years before He appeared among men He revealed His purpose in prophecy: "See then, I said, I am coming to fulfill what is written of Me, where the book lies unrolled; to do Thy will, O My God, is all My desire, to carry out that law of Thine which is written in My Heart." (Ps. 39:8).

Christ made this prophecy His own when He said:

"For I have descended from heaven not to do My own will but the will of Him who sent Me." (John 6:38). How much more then, should we make this our first lesson from Christ, our Model! If Christ, who is God, came down from heaven to do the will of His Father, then we, the object of His Mission, have been created to do the will of His Father.

To him who sees this and believes it, Christ becomes not only the Model, but the Way, the Truth, and the Life. That is, through Christ alone he has the power to do God's will, through Christ alone he obtains the knowledge of God's will, through Christ alone he lives in God.

And what happens as a result? Every thought and word and act of his life takes on a different aspect. He has only one motive for all he does: the love of God and the desire to do His will. He has only one attitude toward all that is done to him. All things are under God's complete control and so are to be accepted with gratitude as from the hand of God.

His incentive to do his best is increased one hundredfold. His pride of achievement has vanished and is replaced by humble acknowledgement that no results are possible except by the power of God; that no work is successful except that done as by a faithful instrument in God's hands. He recalls constantly Christ's gentle but firm reminder: "He who abides in Me and I in him, he it is who bears much fruit; because apart from Me you can product nothing." (John 15:5).

Pride, vainglory, jealousy, contentiousness, cannot possibly exist in the soul who with St. Paul refers all his works: "to Him who is able by His power working in us to do far more than we can either ask or think, to Him be the glory in the Church and in Christ Jesus for all the generations of eternity. Amen." (Eph. 3:20-21).

But even more precious for the peace of soul of the one who makes Christ his model, is his attitude toward all that happens to him in his relationship with others. One whose only motive is to do the will of Christ cannot possibly be vexed at anything that others do, even those which may seem to be directly contrary to all that he has been trying to do. He remembers that Christ loves each soul, even those whose actions may clash with his own.

Look at the example Christ gives us here! He loved even the most wicked sinners, however much He may have hated their sins. No amount of sin caused Him to turn His back on those who, be their sins, had driven Him out of their own hearts. On the contrary, He stood ready to forgive even Judas after he made himself Christ's bitter enemy.

From the human viewpoint, Christ's entire ministry was a colossal failure. He went about doing good. He offered His generous love and His healing touch to all who would come to Him in this world — and everlasting happiness for those who would follow His example of conformity to the will of God. Yet, from most of those to whom He preached this goodness, He received only hatred and contempt and injustice and persecution which culminated in the tragedy of ingratitude enacted on the Cross, when even those whom He had chosen as His closest friends left Him to die almost alone.

What could be added to make His failure more complete! Yet every minute He was God, working in complete union of will with God the Father and God the Holy Spirit. The result He achieved was the perfect fulfillment of the divine plan for the Salvation of the world. But to this day, it is a stumbling-block to those who will not see it with the eye of Faith.

But those who will believe find that it can remove the last vestige of anxiety or vexation over the apparent perversity of those with whom they have to live and work, or of those whom we must obey because God has placed them as superiors over us. It should make every community find a new incentive for mutual love, patience, forbearance and peace. It should put joy in all that we do to obey God's will as it is made know to us from day to day, even though apparent failure or ill-success may follow from our faithful performance of our duty. It should make us utterly immune to discouragement from opposition or interference, either from persons or things or from our own frailty. Always we will rest secure in the knowledge that we are pleasing God as long as we are oblivious of all else but God's holy will!

We should always rejoice that Christ, our Model, is so easily available to us. As St. Paul says: "He is the First-born of many brethren." (Rom. 8:29). Christ, our Brother, has the power to turn all our failure into success and: "He is able for all time to save those who come to God through Him, since He is always living to intercede for them." (Heb. 7:25).

Christ, our Model, according to the saintly Abbot Marmion is: "The revelation of God adapted to our weakness. He is God living amongst us and showing us by His tangible human life how we ought to live in order to please our Father in heaven." (Christ the Ideal, p. 24).

And this is what Christ tells us: "I have not spoken from Myself; on the contrary; the Father who sent Me has Himself given Me a command what to say and what to declare. And I know that His command is eternal life. Whatever I speak, therefore, I speak just as the Father has bidden Me." (John 12:49). Do we need any further recommendation to urge us to conform our lives to the example Christ has given us?

How paltry then, is all that we can do by our own cleverness or industry or ambition or craft! If it is done apart from Christ, we have no power to do anything. Yet even our failure is eminently successful when it is sustained by Him who said: "Take My yoke upon you, and learn of Me, for I am gentle and humble of heart; and you shall find rest for your souls. For My yoke is easy and My burden light." (Matt. 11:29).

Not only is He the divine and perfect Model for our imitation in every virtue, but He is the God who has the love for us and the power to make our life a success if we live our life in Him by the Sacraments, by doing all that we do for love of Him, and by constant union with Him in prayer. "He who abides in Me and I in him, he it is who bears abundant fruit."

Study Questions:

1. Reproduce the trend of thought which stems from the quotation of the words of Christ which end with the sentence: "Do you therefore be perfect as your heavenly Father is perfect."

2. Briefly describe the eight *beatitudes* proposed by Christ in His Sermon on the Mount.

3. Elaborate the thoughts of a Catholic or non-Catholic who wishes to conform to the will of God, in considering Christ's own fulfillment of the admonition to be perfect-as-God-is-perfect.

4. Compare these thoughts with the opposite ones which make a stumbling-block for the worldly minded.

5. Elaborate the sentence: "We know that the superabundant suffering of Christ had a twofold purpose" and discuss the details.

6. Develop the answer to this question: "If we are moved by the compelling motive to take Christ for our Model, what is the first thing we should observe that is to be copied?"

7. Discuss the result in the soul of the one who thus takes Christ for his Model.

8. Discuss the example of Christ in His attitude toward sinners.

9. Comment on the sentence: "From the human viewpoint, Christ's entire ministry was a colossal failure."

10. Show how this "failure" brought about the perfect fulfillment of God's purpose for those who do make Christ their Model.

CHAPTER XIV

MARY, A MODEL

There is one "difficulty" or obstacle often experienced by non-Catholics which "cradle-Catholics" find equally difficult to understand when it is manifested by a word or act of the non-Catholic. The difficulty arises from the veneration by the Catholic world of the Blessed Virgin Mary. The manifestation which Catholics find hard to understand, appears in the coolness or indifference or out-right hostility toward this practice which is felt by most Protestant Christians.

Many non-Catholics believe that Catholics offer divine worship to the Blessed Virgin. Since she is obviously a creature, this constitutes in their minds, contemptible idolatry on the part of Catholics. On the other hand, it never occurs to Catholics to realize that their behavior toward the Blessed Virgin looks like idolatry to one who is a stranger to the Catholic doctrine regarding the status of Mary in the divine economy of worship. It is with a present sense of humble apology toward our Blessed Mother, that I can remember my own reactions as a non-Catholic and do no less than admit that each is at least partly justified in his attitude.

In fact, it was not until I became a Catholic myself that I began to see that the true Catholic is so steeped in the knowledge that the Triune God alone has title to the exclusive worship of adoration, that it never occurs to him to think that his expression of love for the Mother of

God-the-Son is anything else than a reflection of his worship of her Son.

It was only then that it began to dawn on me that the
close intimacy between heaven-with-all-its-saints, and the
souls of us wayfarers here on earth, makes it seem perfectly natural to one who has been raised in the Faith to
go down on his knees before a statue of the Blessed
Virgin or a saint whom he knows to be in heaven. This he
does without the slightest thought of adoration of any
one but God, the Creator of the wood or stone of the
image, as well as the soul and body of the person represented, who has now become especially dear to God.

This misunderstanding stems from a difference in the
appreciation of the relationship between the immortal
soul of a Christian, and the ocean of God's omnipotence
which surrounds him and envelops him and all the
material world around him. He is hemmed in, one might
say, by his physical senses as the only windows of perception. While God's omnipotence *is* manifested by the
material world, it is not perceptible to the senses except
as they are illuminated by the intellect. The height of perception comes to the senses only when they are also fortified by the light of supernatural grace.

The Catholic is, or should be, so accustomed to this
spiritual perception of God's presence in all that his
senses convey to his mind, that the veil between God and
himself in every creature, including his own person, seems
so very thin that he has no trouble in acknowledging it
and respecting it with admiration and wonder.

A faint idea of the thinness of the veil between the
senses and the transcendent divine presence may be
hinted in the use of our organ of sight, the marvelous
human eye. At noon-day our soul is informed through
this precious instrument, of all the beauties of created
nature around us. It not only discloses all the intricate
detail of the foreground, but easily spans the ninety-odd

millions of miles of space which separate us from the source of light which permits the eye to function.

But let us go abroad on a star-lit midnight, when the crass power of the sun no longer limits the capacity of our vision and — behold! we see perhaps one-hundred-million times as far — the stars! When this last flicker of contact between the senses and the Truth is dimmed at death, our souls may then perceive how God holds it all in being as in the hollow of His hand.

But what has this to do with the reason for the mis-understanding of the non-Catholic as to the behavior of the Catholic toward the Blessed Virgin Mary? It has everything to do with it! The Catholic has ingrained in the fiber of his being an intimacy with the reality of the invisible supernatural presence of God. He knows of God's presence in every particle of the material world. He knows that this presence is what keeps it from dropping back into nothingness.

But far more poignantly does he sense God's presence in every human soul whom God has endowed with those qualities of intelligence and free-will which reflect most nearly the image of God. He knows that, by the power of God, the souls of those who have graduated from this life into heaven are made aware, not only of the reality of God as He is, but also of those things in the world which God wishes them to know.

It would never occur to him to doubt that this is very specially true of the Blessed Virgin, since he knows that God has reunited her soul and body so that she is now in the glorious state which we will enjoy after the Resurrec-tion of the dead. And so he does not hesitate to address prayers to her with perfect assurance that God makes them known to her. He also believes that God wishes him to turn to her for help, since God gave her to us as our heavenly Queen and Mother.

He knows that by herself alone, she has no more power than any other creature to hear his prayers or to do anything about them if she did. He would be horrified at the thought of offering the homage of worship to her as if she or her image had any divine power independent of God.

And that brings us to another reason for the Catholic's veneration of the Blessed Virgin, which is hard for the non-Catholic to understand. This reason is so tremendous that the simple statement of it sounds inadequate. It is that the Catholic believes that Mary became, really and truly, the Mother of God.

This one fact accounts for all the rest and makes her different and more precious to God and to man than any other creature that ever lived. But for this, you and I would never have heard of the little daughter of St. Joachuim and St. Ann. But because of this, Mary was able to say with certainty: "All generations shall call me blessed, for to me the Almighty hath done wonders, and Holy is His Name! "

Stop for a moment and meditate on this one fact! If the Catholic's belief is literally true, there really can be no further possible reason for the non-Catholic's surprise at, or objection to, the Catholic's attitude or behavior toward her as I have explained it. Certainly there could be no greater dignity bestowed upon a human being than to become the human instrument whereby almighty God chose to take upon Himself our human nature, and bring His divinity into the realm of our sense knowledge.

And so it certainly comes about by the mysterious Providence of God, that the relationship between every human soul and this Mother of God should be one of profound respect and veneration of her exalted status among men; of humble admiration of her unparalleled devotion to the will of God; of sincere emulation of her supreme example of Christian perfection; of hopeful acknowledgment of her preeminent influence as a mediatrix of graces from her divine Son who deigned to make Himself subject to this creature of His predilection during His childhood and, lastly and most specially, of fervent filial love trust and confidence in her mother's love for himself.

All this is ratified and confirmed by our Lord's words from the Cross, declaring her to be the Mother of every soul united with Christ to become thereby adopted sons of God the Father.

Whatever the non-Catholic may find it in his heart to believe regarding the Mother of God, this explanation should, at least, make him understand that the Catholic is not guilty of blasphemous idolatry when he prays to God through the intercession of her upon whom God has showered so many evidences of his love. In fact, having this belief, the Catholic would be guilty of shocking ingratitude if he did not acknowledge his veneration of her as a God-chosen channel of His love.

Now it comes to mind that many non-Catholic Christians recite that declaration of belief, handed down to them from the Apostles, called the Apostles' Creed, which contains these words: "I believe in God the Father almighty, Creator of heaven and earth, and in Jesus Christ His only Son, our Lord, Who was conceived by the Holy Spirit, born of the Virgin Mary". . . What is the difference, then, between the belief of the Catholic and that of the non-Catholic Christian who subscribes to the Apostles' Creed? The only plausible answer lies in the examination of the different thought concepts behind this declaration of faith.

It will perhaps make my meaning more clear if I quote what one very large group of non-Catholic Christians said about their own interpretation of the answer to this question. I quote from the report of the "Commission on Christian Doctrine" appointed by the Anglican Archbishops of Canterbury and York, which, after fourteen years of deliberation, published in 1938 a book entitled: "The Doctrine of the Church of England." Regarding the acceptance of the three creeds to which the Church of

England subscribes, their comment is as follows: "It is not therefore illegitimate to accept and affirm particular clauses of the Creeds while understanding them in a symbolic sense." The word "symbolic" is later defined as meaning: "Pictorial expressions of spiritual truths, even though the supposed facts themselves did not actually happen."

This makes it clear that one can be a member in good standing of the Anglican Church, and recite the Apostles' Creed, while believing that the Incarnation of a divine Person by birth from a virgin mother "did not actually happen."

It should, however, be equally clear that such a declaration of doctrine authorized by the head of the Catholic Church, would instantly destroy the faith of every Catholic alive! This would happen because absolute infallible certainty as to the contents of the Deposit of Faith, is the *sine-qua-non* of the existence of the Catholic Church.

Such a declaration would, for a Catholic, be a repudiation of the Creeds which, for nineteen centuries, have formed the very core of the Deposit of Faith. This would be an admission of the error of the former doctrine and so would nullify every other claim of the Church. Indeed, this very item of faith precisely marks the difference between a Catholic and every one else in the world.

On the other hand, this application of the term *symbolic*, as defined by the Anglican Commission on Christian Doctrine, is the only reasonable basis for denial of the very definite revelations made by Christ as to the unity, stability, infallibility, indefectibility and catholicity of His Church. It therefore becomes the *sine-qua-non* of the existence of the non-Catholic Christian Churches.

The clear statement of this fact should, however, enable each to understand the other better. Whatever the non-Catholic may believe, he will see that the behavior of the Catholic in honoring the Blessed Virgin is consistent with his belief that she is really and truly the Mother of God.

Catholics love Mary because she was the instrumental cause of bringing us God in Person. As we say in her Litany, she is the "Cause of our joy." For us she needs no other recommendation. One glance at the Church's calendar of feasts confirms our knowledge from God Himself that He wishes her to be loved and venerated by all who profess to love Him.

By all this honor to her, the Church wishes to teach us to seek the help, the example and the encouragement which Christ wishes us to obtain through His Mother. Mary should be dearer to every human soul than any other human person, since God gave her to us as our Mother and the Mediatrix of graces for us.

But what I want more than all else to gain for you by this knowledge is a keen desire to use the help she is so ready to give to each one of us. No one who has been spiteful or mean or careless of others or a detractor or slanderer or jealous or selfish or suspicious or sullen or gossiping or murmuring — has any real claim to help from our Mother. Why? Because all these indignities shown to one's associates, who are her children, have been insults to her and to her Son. And yet, she, who has a greater claim to dignity than any other woman alive, has proven by her humility that she is ready to forgive all slights to her and to help you to become like her. She is the one who can and will obtain for you the grace of humility, courage, charity, to trample on the self-love which may stand in the way of an immediate change in the way of life that you have allowed yourself to fall into. How do I know? Because for almost two thousand years she had done it so many times and for so many people even worse than we are, that she can do it in our case without even bothering to ask for a miracle.

"But," you say, "there are some mean things done by my neighbors that certainly ask for retaliation. And some people are so negligent and so careless and so absent-minded and so tardy and so out-of-tune in general, and so selfish, that somebody has to do something about it." I answer: "All that is going to be changed now. You are going to like it no matter how bad it seems. You are going to try to behave toward all these things as the Blessed Virgin would behave, and really mean it."

The natural man or the little boy or girl in us is always centered on self and rebels against everything that is not exactly according to our pleasure. But our dear Mother says: "No. Your pleasure must be to do the will of my Son, to be abandoned to His will, to love even your enemy because He loves them even though He hates their sins. You are trying to learn to love Him. Please don't spoil it all by holding grudges or failing in Charity toward your neighbor. Before you act or speak, learn to ask yourself: 'Would my Mother do it this way?' Would she say to you: 'Do you think I planned to get even with those who closed their doors on me at Bethlehem?'"

I very much dislike discourses about the Blessed Virgin based on the imagination of the writer. It is true that there is not very much specific information about her. But to my mind God did not bring that about in order to invite us to invent an avalanche of sweet nonsense about her that has no better than an even chance of being true.

We know plenty about her for sure to fill every lifetime with admiration, not only to call her "blessed" but to give us the determination to make her our model and advocate for grace to do as she would have us do.

We know for sure her utter charity and sinlessness because she placed God, not just first, but all-in-all. We know for sure her perfect humility, simplicity, obedience, courage. Summed up – we know for sure her perfect abandonment to God's will.

What more do we need to make us know it than this: One night at Bethlehem, when the Precious Child was less than two years old, Joseph told her that they must leave that night, on foot for Egypt, over two-hundred miles of almost waterless desert; through country that no one would ordinarily dare to attempt except in an armed caravan, to a destination where the people would be utter strangers, hostile to the Jewish people and ignorant of their language; to stay for an unknown length of time; with no passport except a dream vision which was reported to Mary by Joseph.

Joseph had said that the Child's life was in danger. Human prudence would have called it an impossible situation. I have been over part of the route they took. I doubt if you have ever seen anything worse. Except for Joseph's word, the Child's life would appear to be far safer in Bethlehem! But they left! They left that night — for Egypt — and they remained there until Herod was dead.

There is one other event that, to my mind, is all we should need to make each one of us resolve to heed from Mary the last words reported of her in the Bible. These words were spoken at the very beginning of the ministry of her Son, when she had finished her part in delivering Him to the world. It was at the Marriage Feast at Cana, when her host was in trouble because of the shortage of wine. It was then that God was to show the world that He would never refuse a petition addressed to Him through Mary. Her words were these: "Whatever He bids you do, do it." (John 2:5).

Study Questions:

1. Explain the misunderstanding regarding "Mary-Worship" from the viewpoint of the non-Catholic and make it understandable to the Catholic.

2. Explain the author's discovery, upon becoming a Catholic, of the true relationship between us wayfarers and the saints and comment on the manifestation of that relationship.

3. Comment on the hint of the thinness of the veil between the physical senses and the transcendent divine presence suggested by the author as to the organ of sight, the eye, and apply it to the behavior of Catholics toward the Blessed Virgin Mary.

4. Comment on the greatest of all the reasons for veneration of the Blessed Virgin and describe the attitude which it should generate in us.

5. Account for the difference in the non-Catholic interpretation of the clause in the Apostles Creed which specifies belief in: "Jesus Christ His only Son, our Lord, Who was conceived by the Holy Spirit, born of the Virgin Mary –" as explained by the Anglican Church.

6. Explain what would be the effect of this interpretation if it were made within the Catholic Church.

7. What should be the net result to us, here and now, of this status of the Blessed Virgin Mary?

8. Elaborate the author's statement: "Mary should be dearer to every human soul than any other human person, since God gave her to us as our Mother and the Mediatrix of graces for us."

9. Give Our Lady's answer to the all-too-human inclination to depart from her example and her counsel.

10. Recount the sequel to Joseph's dream at Bethlehem that proves Our Lady's title to our utter loyalty and trust.

CHAPTER XV

PATIENCE IS POSITIVE

The most sublime and soul-satisfying aspect of the counsel given by Christ to His immediate and intimate friends seems always to center around complete and loving trust in divine Providence. Christ's emphasis on these virtues of trust and hope appears most often when He is stirred by thy contrast of the very opposite qualities in many of the leaders of those who were plotting His death. Their grudging attitude toward God and their jealous greed for power and special privilege made them Christ's implacable enemies.

Their cold and calculating cavil over trivialities, such as shelling out wheat in the hand on the Sabbath, seems to have been the setting planned by God to make the serenity of Christ's new teaching stand out in all its gracious perfection. It is strange, however, that almighty God should seem to have to try so hard to make us see that we are perfectly safe when we leave everything to Him. Why should He have to coax us to see that we are decidedly *unsafe* whenever we fail to heed these admonitions. One would think that God would need no special pleading to inspire confidence. And yet, this too, may be a part of God's plan to make its blessing all the more precious to those who will see and believe.

St. Luke's Gospel seems to have been given this subtle atmosphere in a high degree by the gentle inspiration of the Holy Spirit. There is a part of this Gospel which

Scripture scholars call St. Luke's "major insertion." It falls between chapters ten and eighteen. The matter of this part seems to alternate between the expression of the venom of hate on the part of the Scribes and Pharisees, and Christ's denunciation of their attitude. This leads up to Christ's loving exposition of the doctrine of abandonment to the Providence of God.

The early part of St. Luke's major insertion introduces a new phase of Christ's teaching. He had just finished a scathing denunciation of the Pharisees and the Doctors of the Law in which He brought down upon them the guilt of all the murders of God's ministers, the prophets, who had tried in the past to keep God's chosen race from going astray. He then turned to the large crowd which had, as usual, gathered to witness His masterful circumvention of the guile of these evil workers of iniquity.

And here begins Christ's most compelling invitation to be, not just attentive to God's good pleasure, but to orient the whole of one's life around the adequacy of God's management of every single minute of it. It applies not only to the great and important events which mark the difference between success or failure in life, but to every detail, even the things that happen that are as trivial as the death of a sparrow.

Christ begins this discourse with the following exclamation: *"And I say this to you who are My friends: Do not be afraid of those who can kill the body and after that can do no more. I will tell you who it is you must fear: Fear him who has power not only to kill but to cast a man into hell: Yes I tell you, fear him."* (Luke 12:4-5).

One might have expected Him to save it for the climax at the end, since it emphasizes the greatest possible contrast between the power of God and the power of man. "Fear Him who has power not only to kill but to cast into hell." In other words, the very limit of man's power to injure is the separation of body and soul by murder. But this power need not cause the slightest anxiety to one who knows that his soul is safe in God's keeping. The *only* thing in this life which such a one need fear is an act or example which might cheat him of that protection of God.

With this as a starting point, Christ goes on to show how this filial fear of God which expresses itself in loving abandonment, is rewarded by the removal of every *cause* for fear. Those who are not so fortunate as to have placed themselves entirely in God's hands are beset with constant fear of a very different kind.

This adequacy of God's care of those who make themselves God's friends, is shown by Christ to include all our needs without exception. Here is a sample of it: "Observe the ravens how they neither sow nor reap; they have no storehouse nor barn; yet God feeds them. Of how much more value are you than the birds! ... And as for you — do not be seeking what to eat, or what to drink, nor be in anxious suspense; for the nations of the world seek after all these things; but your Father knows that you need them. Seek instead His Kingdom, and these things shall be given you besides." (Luke 12:24-31).

This beautiful lesson of God's perfect success in managing the balance of nature in His feeding of the ravens and His adornment of the lilies of the field without any care on the part of these creatures, brings home to His disciples the folly of anxiety about the material needs of life; about food and clothing and shelter. Even anxiety about death inself is wasted energy which one might very much better spend in keeping one's self ready for death by doing always the will of God, knowing that then; "All these things shall be given you besides."

It is not, however, until somewhat later in His teaching of His disciples that Christ tells them what might be called the formula for placing themselves in this happy condition of being provided for in every detail by the Providence of God. He leads them by many beautiful parables to see that self-renunciation is the immediate fruit of this abandonment to God, and that material wealth is apt to be a misleading influence. Finally, after picturing the sad plight of those who resist God's dominion as the end of the world approaches, He gives the disciples the key whereby they will remain safe even when called upon to meet the most bitter and wicked persecution that the world has ever seen. He says: "And you shall be hated by all for My Name's sake; yet not a hair of your head shall perish. By your *patience* you shall win your souls." (Luke 21:18-19).

By your patience you shall win! It is this aspect of patience as the positive key to success in competition with evil that has given me a clue toward the development of a technique for the conquest of mental trials. Immediately when I began to study the virtue of patience, I began to discover a "brand-new" appreciation for this most useful tool of those who wish to know how to practice true and joyful abandonment to divine Providence.

I had previously accepted the idea of patience as a sort of resignation in the face of the unavoidable. I had associated this virtue with the idea that if no relief could be found, it is virtuous to "grin and bear it." Or, as those who like to think of themselves as martyrs would have it: "to suffer in silence." But it now appears that that is the very thing which modern psychiatry says is the source of all the tensions and anxieties which cause our insides to misbehave with manifestations of peptic ulcers, arthritis, asthma, hay fever, even angina and high blood pressure.

Of course, it is virtuous to accept the unavoidable with resignation. It is also true that such action is included in the practice of patience. But the notion that started me to couple the idea of *peace* with that of patience was the discovery that theologians classify patience as an ally of the *cardinal* virtue of Fortitude, and the realization that that is precisely what it is. The very meaning of the words "cardinal" and "fortitude" suggest action rather than just acceptance.

Before I began the study of Latin (at age fifty-three), I used to think that the word "cardinal," when applied to virtues, meant a sort of underlining in red-ink to emphasize that they should be given special attention. But the idea of action in that word is still more emphatic, since it signifies the *hinge* upon which the door of spiritual progress swings open. It is not functioning as a hinge if it is merely holding the door shut! It must open and go out to meet whatever is in opposition in order to qualify as a hinge.

In exactly the same connotation of positive action, the virtue of Fortitude is defined by Father Tanquerey as: "a supernatural moral virtue that strengthens the soul in the *pursuit* of difficult moral good without allowing it to be deterred by fear, even the fear of death." (Tan. par. 1076).

Patience is that brand of Fortitude which, as Tanquerey continues, "makes us withstand with equanimity of soul, for the love of God, and in union with Jesus Christ, all physical and moral suffering." (Tan. par. 1088). The perfection of this virtue is exemplified by our Lord Himself as Victim at His entrance into the world. He even desired and sought for His Passion to manifest His love for those who put their trust in Him. "And I have a baptism wherewith I am to be baptized. And how I am straightened until it is accomplished." (Luke 12:50).

The classic example of patience, pictured for us by the inspiration of the Holy Spirit, is the Old Testament character of Job. God gave him a victory over untold suffering because of his declaration of abandonment to the will of God: "Though He slay me, yet will I put my trust in Him." (Job 13:15).

This notion of the positive character of patience is no new invention. It goes right back to Christ Himself. In the vivid parable of the Sower, He compares the seed that fell on good soil to: "Those who with a noble and generous heart, having heard the word, hold it fast and yield fruit with *patience*." (Luke 8:15). "By your patience you shall win your souls." (21:9).

St. Cyprian in the third century, extols patience with these words: "It is patience which makes us pleasing to God and keeps us in His service: which calms our anger, checks our tongue, rules our mind, keeps the peace, controls discipline, breaks the violence of passion, represses the outburst of pride, extinguishes hatred and strife, checks the power of riches, refreshes the needy, protects the undivided love of the espoused and married, makes us humble in prosperity, brave in adversity, and meek in the face of injuries." If this is a fair encomium of this precious branch of the cardinal virtue of Fortitude, what more do we need to secure perfection in any vocation leading to heaven? But still St. Cyprian continues: "It teaches us to forgive those who injure us. It triumphs over temptations readily, endures persecutions and crowns martyrdom. This it is which firmly fortifies the foundations of our Faith! "

The only connection between these sentiments and that pessimistic admonition to "grin and bear it" is to put the accent on the "grin." Our Faith gives us plenty of reason to smile instead of sharing with other men the "fear of what is coming upon the world."

Indeed, it was in preparation for Christ's dire predictions of anxiety of men's minds at the approach of the end of the world that He fortified His chosen ones with the assurance: "Not a hair of your heads shall perish. By your patience you shall win your souls." (Luke 21:18-19). Then followed the details which would: "Make men pine away with fear and apprehension of what is coming upon the world, for the forces of heaven shall be disturbed... But when these events begin to come to pass, look up and lift up your heads because your redemption is drawing near." (Luke 21:26-28).

Now, the situation for which Christ was preparing His disciples during the first three centuries of persecution and martyrdom, and the situation which souls will face at the end of the world, is no different from our situation in this very day. The setting in which we live today offers the same contrast — helplessness of those who have nothing but weapons of war to offer mankind; peace and confidence of those who know for certain that every detail of the world's history and future is directed by the omniscient hand of almighty God.

In fact, the situation today gives ample cause for men's hearts to "wither in fear of what is coming upon the world." It also gives double reason for *us* who know the truth, to practice that positive patience whereby we, in conforming to God's will, can win our souls and firmly fortify the foundations of our Faith!

It would really be highly amusing, if it were not at the same time tragically pitiful, that the two principal fears which harass the minds of the militant materialists of today are — one: the extermination of the human race by atomic warfare and, two: the swarming multiplication of the human race by "un-planned" parenthood. A recent issue of one of the news-magazines contained an article in which it was predicted with grave concern that within a few hundred years the entire land area of the world would be covered with human beings. No hope of relief was suggested unless those trying to prevent this disaster by means of abortion, contraception, and sterilization should succeed in overcoming the obstruction still encountered in superstition, folk-customs, old wives tales, and — oh yes, authentic religious belief.

The anxiety of these people stems from their fear that *chance* which, they assume, has successfully brought the world through the billions of years of its sweetly ordered development until now, is at last facing its Waterloo unless man, the most precious product of *chance*, can come to its rescue by upsetting the hitherto successful order of nature.

Those of us for whom "patience firmly fortifies the foundation of our faith in God," are quite aware that the possibility of atomic extinction as well as the possibility of too many neighbors, *may* signal the approach of the end of the world. In fact, if they do not, we might say that we will be missing two very fine opportunities to end it all. *But* we who also know that it is God, and not Chance, who has brought the world to its present intricate state of balance and perfection, are perfectly serene in the certain knowledge that, if God wishes to have the world support the human race for another billion years. He will see that it does so!

But our present sense of security, the fruit of positive patience, stems from the knowledge that it will not be God's mismanagement of the world that will bring about its end. On the contrary, it will be God's final intervention when the forces of evil have multiplied disobedience to a point beyond which God's toleration will not go!

The laws against contraception, sterilization, abortion or any other kind of murder, are God's laws, not those of the Catholic Church. They bind all men equally, not just Catholics. The penalty for violation involves no fine or imprisonment. In fact, violation will probably go on increasing until the end of the world. Such is the patience of God.

Catholics, however, who practice positive patience to fortify their faith, will do all they can to protect the innocent from those who are misguided or maliciously evil, and will pray for the latter, that God will have mercy on their souls and bring them to see their folly!

Meanwhile, we should be supremely happy that we do not have to share their anxiety. We have Christ's definite word for it that we need have no fear of those who are only able to kill the body by atom-bomb, or by germ-warfare, or any other devilment. Nor do we need fear those who would lead us into sin by scandal – *provided* that by patience we cling firmly to Him who *can* save the soul from being cast into hell. It is, however, part of the duty of abandonment to God's will to work for and pray for the conversion of those who would seek to kill us or to cause the ruin of our souls.

The plight of those who do not have this assurance of resting secure in God's loving Providence is very sad and very real. It will undoubtedly become more terrific as the human race plunges on in its mad determination to depart from God's Law. It is part of the price of our peace and serenity in all this turmoil that we never cease working as God's instruments in their behalf. "Fear not, little flock, for it hath pleased your Father to give you a kingdom . . . make yourselves purses which will not grow old, an inexhaustible treasure in heaven, where neither thief approaches nor moth destroys. For where your treasure is, there will your heart be also." (Luke 12:32-34).

Study Questions:

1. Elaborate and contrast with its opposite the opening sentence of this chapter: "The most sublime and soul-satisfying aspect of the counsel given by Christ to His immediate and intimate friends seems always to center around the complete and loving trust in Divine Providence."

2. Christ invites each one to orientate his life around the adequacy of God's management of every single minute of it. He says: "Do not be afraid of those who can kill the body and after that can do no more." Elaborate on this sentence.

3. Describe Christ's lesson of God's perfect success in managing the balance of nature and tell its application to all of us.

4. Explain how Christ's words: "By your *Patience* you shall win your souls" gives the key to safety against persecution and evil.

5. Explain the false concept of patience which psychiatrists warn against and correct it by relating it to the Cardinal Virtue of Fortitude.

6. Give Father Tanquerey's definition of *Fortitude* and tell how *Patience* is one brand of Fortitude exemplified by Christ.

7. Quote the parable of the Sower and St. Cyprian to show the positive character of *Patience*.

8. Discuss this sentence of the text: "The situation for which Christ was preparing His disciples during the first three centuries of persecution and martyrdom and the situation which souls will face at the end of the world, is no different from our situation in this very day."

9. Discuss the materialists' dilemma over the world's progress governed by "chance", and reconcile the believer's composure.

10. What should be the behavior of those of us who face what could be the end of the world in these days of strife?

CHAPTER XVI

MAN'S PART IN CREATION:
SIN — SORROW — SUFFERING
THE PROBLEM OF EVIL

Two things should be obvious to the adult human mind of the man or woman who looks without prejudice at this universe. First, the overwhelming evidence of order in the operation of all things, denies the possibility of *chance* and demands the recognition of intelligent design coupled with power free from limitation, and so in complete control of all that is in being. Second, a modicum of disorder which would upset the whole of creation, were it not also under the complete control of the Designer and so subject to the infinity of His wisdom, even though beyond the understanding of human reason alone.

This is a statement in philosophical language of the *Problem of Evil* which confronts every child of Adam born into the world. Reason alone cannot supply a perfect explanation for the toleration of sin, sorrow and suffering in a world dominated by a personal omnipotent God of love. The fact, however, that they are in the world, coupled with the fact of the otherwise perfect order in the world, does suggest to the intellect of man that they are tolerated for a reason that is compatible with the infinite perfection of the Creator.

It is also apparent to reason that the precious power and freewill possessed by man, make him the only visible creature capable of responsibility for this upsetting influence. All else obeys the laws of its nature because it cannot do otherwise. Man alone can violate these laws by the misuse of his free will. He cannot, however, avoid responsibility for his violation. He may deny it, but he cannot avoid the knowledge that he is guilty of sin.

It is easy to see, however, that reason alone is not a strong weapon in the hands of the individual human being when confronted with the tragic manifestations of sin, sorrow and suffering which appear to beset innocent victims all along the path of history. So part of the Problem of Evil itself has been the devastating doubt that it generates in the hearts of men and women sharing in or observing this apparent contradiction of divine protection of those who love God. Its most evil manifestation, then, is that it forms a barrier that keeps some men from God.

If reason alone were the only source of solution of the Problem of Evil, it might partially explain why men and women all down the centuries have made it an excuse to rebel against God, to "curse God and die," to defy the evidence of His existence, to resist the action of His Grace. Catholics and non-Catholics alike have allowed themselves to be guilty of this distrust of God on the pretext that one form or another of the Problem of Evil makes it impossible for them to believe in a merciful all-powerful God of love.

I said, if reason alone were the *only* source of solution it *might* be a *partial* explanation of this tragic cause of man's defection. But, from the very beginning of man's existence, reason has never been left alone. God the Creator has given us His own word and explanation of the reason for evil and suffering in the world. There is no mystery concerning God's management of the universe of His creation more definitely explained by revelation, and guaranteed by God Himself. Man may say that, in his opinion, evil and suffering are incompatible with the notion of a merciful, loving, omnipotent God. But he cannot reasonably say that God has not made it abundantly clear that such an opinion is wrong.

Not only has God's revelation made it clear that all the suffering in the world is the result of sin, but He has shown that man's sin is the reason for dislocation of order in the material world which makes suffering universal and not a mere punishment proportioned to individual sin, administered to the individual sinner.

In the third chapter of the Book of Genesis we find God's word that the human race has not only been deprived by the sin of our first parents, of the preternatural gifts of bodily immortality and freedom from suffering and integrity of free will, but that all man's material surroundings are subjected to the same curse. This brings the effects of sin into the lives of innocent victims while leaving the individual sinner sometimes untouched. "Now through thy act the very ground is under a curse . . . Dust thou art and unto dust thou shalt return." (Gen. 3:17-19).

St. Paul, a realist if there ever was one, has impressed into the New Testament this same revelation of the mystery of man's suffering of evil in the material world: "Creation," he says, "was subjected to futility – not by any will of its own, but because of Him who subjected it – in hope that even creation itself shall be set free from the servitude of decay into the glorious liberty of the children of God. For we know that all creation groans and agonizes together until now; and not only it, but ourselves, who possess. the first fruits of the Spirit, even we ourselves groan inwardly, awaiting our adoption – the redemption of our body." (Rom. 8:20-23).

But how often one hears the moan: "How can you possibly say that a good and loving and merciful and all-powerful God exists who allows my innocent baby to be burned to death, my darling wife to suffer agony for months or years and then die in the prime of youth; my children to starve because my husband was shot by a thief who robbed us; my baby to have been born without the faculty of reason; my son to be born whom you say will be subjected to eternal punishment in hell if he dies unrepentant in a state of grave sin? Myself to go through life begging God on my knees for relief from this evil that I hate, and never a sign of relief? "

Part of the proof of the rightness of the acknowledgement of a good God who permits the Problem of Evil, is the very fact that we cannot know its answer completely in this world. Nothing can be more obvious than God's jealous insistence upon the preservation of man's free will, that gift which most nearly reflects God's own perfection, and which raises man to a dignity above all the rest of material creation.

God asks man's belief in Him and trust in Him and love of Him by an act of man's free will, aided, to be sure, by grace and revelation, made in the face of some incompletely answered questions. The Problem of Evil embraces all these questions and offers an answer sufficient for acceptance by reason and clinched by revelation. Man is always free to reject the answers, but he cannot deny that they are there.

God will not prevent man from using his free will to commit sin. If He did, it would mean that man, by his free will could constrain God to act in obedience to the will of His creature, and thus place a limit on God's unlimited exercise of *His* free will.

It follows then, that God expects us to believe Him and to trust Him, not because we are *compelled* by reason, but because He has told us the Truth.

The obvious purpose of the Old Testament Book of Job is to show the reward given by God for the trust and submission of Job to God's will, in spite of the untold suffering of this innocent man. We are reminded again of this by St. James in the New Testament. He says: "You have heard of the patience of Job and seen how the Lord finally dealt with him; for the Lord is full of compassion and is merciful." (James 5:10).

St. Paul also expresses the same command for implicit trust in the mercy of God: "Nay, but who art thou, Oh man, to answer against God? Shall the thing fashioned say to its fashioner, 'Why didst thou make me thus?'" (Roman. 9:20). But nowhere is this same idea expressed with greater beauty than in the eleventh chapter of St. Paul's Epistle to the Romans which was once used for the lesson of Trinity Sunday:

> On the depth of the riches of the wisdom and of the knowledge of God! How incomprehensible are His judgments and how unsearchable His ways! For who hath known the mind of the Lord? Or who hath been His counsellor? Or who hath first given to Him that recompense shall be made to him? For of Him and by Him and in Him are all things: To Him be glory forever! Amen. (Rom. 11:33-36).

The most likely reason, however, for the fact of evil, and the one given a complete answer in revelation, is the evidence it gives of the immensity of the evil of grave sin. God has given man sufficient means to know His will and His infinite lovableness, and sufficient help to enable him to obey God. This was eminently true of our first parents and will always be true of each one of us. To turn against the infinite God by the violation of God's gift of free will, is an act of infinite malice, and each such act could account for all the penalty of evil manifest in the world.

It is strange, too, that man seldom chooses death itself as a reason for complaint against God, or a claim against His love and mercy. Yet the universal penalty of death is the greatest and most obvious of the evil results of Adam's part in the Problem of Evil. But the very universality of death rather than the apparently random distribution of the rest of the Problem of Evil, gives a clue as to the compatibility of evil and God's goodness. It can only mean that God has planned this world as a proving-ground, a training school for something infinitely better

than anything in this world, even if this world were free
from evil.

God has created the world as it is even with His fore-
knowledge that man would seem to spoil it all by intro-
ducing sorrow and suffering through sin. We know by
revelation that it is through the acceptance of suffering
with resignation to God's will and in recognition of His
dominion over all things, that man is perfected. St. Peter
has expressed it thus: "Beloved, do not be surprised at
the fiery trial among you, which comes upon you to test
you, as though a strange thing were befalling you; on the
contrary, rejoice, in so far as you are sharers in the sufferings of the Christ, so that you may be glad and
jubilant at the revelation of His glory." (I Pet. 4:12-14).
And St. Paul adds: "For I hold that the sufferings of the
present time bears no comparison to the glory that is to
be revealed in us." (Rom. 8:18).

But if any doubt could ever linger in the mind of man
as to the revelation regarding the heritage of sin, it is certainly wiped away by the torrent of proof contained in
the revelation of the means of our salvation by the suffering voluntarily accepted by God Himself for our sake.
True, Christ's own Passion and Death, the world's outstanding example of vicarious atonement for sin by acceptance of suffering, was a stumbling-block for many,
but for those who believed, it set the pattern for the perfection of Christian sanctity for all time.

Christ made it clear that His own acceptance of suffering was the efficacious and only acceptable means chosen
by His all-wise Father for adequate atonement for the
guilt of man's sin, to show man the infinite malice involved in his sin, and the infinite love of God for this
wayward creature of His election.

Christ has also made it equally clear that participation
with Him in the glory won by His sacrifice, is conditioned
by acceptance with resignation of whatever trials may be

our lot. These trials must be accepted, not blindly, but with utter trust in God, even though we do not understand His ways. We are told this in Christ's own words: "Blessed are you when men shall revile you and persecute you and say all manner of evil against you falsely for My sake. Be glad and rejoice, because your reward will be abundant in heaven." (Matt. 5:10).

St. Paul repeats the precept of his Master in addressing the Philippians: "For to you it has been granted for the sake of Christ, not only to believe in Him, but also to suffer for His sake." (Phil. 1:29). And to St. Timothy: "If we suffer with Him, we shall also reign with Him. If we die with Him we shall also live with Him." (II Tim. 2:11). "Yes, and all those who wish to live religiously in Christ Jesus are going to be persecuted; while wicked men and impostors will proceed from bad to worse, deceivers of others and themselves deceived." (II Tim.2:13).

And so, sin, sorrow, and suffering make a tragic enigma only for those who refuse to believe the constant teaching of Christ that this world with all its trials, which may seem cruel to our mortal view, only makes sense if it is accepted as God's choice for our preparation for eternal happiness in heaven.

This was indelibly engraved in my heart during the only real trial of my life that involved a brush with the Problem of Evil. As I have told you, I always used to say that Saint Joseph was the only man who had a better wife than mine. And so it was a terrific shock to me to learn that God willed to impose upon her a year of suffering before taking her to Himself at a time of life when all the best years seemed to be ahead.

I have known men and women who have turned such a situation into the only real evil that can happen in this world by rebellion against God, with loss of faith. Thank God, He gave us the grace to see His mercy in giving her a better chance to prepare for death, and so put joy even into suffering in this world. The last year was in many ways the happiest of all, and when the end came the saintly superior of the hospital who was in the room when she died, said to me: "I have been a nurse for twenty-five years and I have heard many prayers for a happy death, but I never felt quite sure that I had seen one until today! "

Those words will burn in my soul as long as I live. They taught me one way to make life a success; namely, so to live that if you are the first to die, the dear ones who remain will be morally certain that God has taken you to heaven! There is no better way to put to rout the Problem of Evil in this world.

Nevertheless, we must not lose sight of the fact that Satan and his evil spirits still wander through the world seeking the ruin of souls. Part of the trust in God which we can exercise in defiance of the Problem of Evil is to deepen our faith in the power of prayer. And so, each one should join in spirit with the priest in the prayers which used to be said in the name of all at the end of Mass, begging God to empower St. Michael to defend us in battle and be our safeguard against the malice and snares of the devil.

Then at last, let us take our stand with St. Paul and say: "Who shall separate us from the love of Christ? Shall affliction, or difficulty, or persecution, or hunger, or nakedness, or danger or sword? ... In all these circumstances we more than conquer through Him who loved us! " (Rom. 8:35-38).

Study Questions:

1. Give (approximately) in philosophical language, a statement of the *Problem of Evil*, and the possibility of reconciling it with God's love.
2. Discuss the source of responsibility for evil and explain what the test calls "its most evil manifestation."
3. Elaborate the sentence: "If reason alone were the *only* source of solution it *might* be a *partial* explanation of the tragic cause of man's defection."
4. Cite two Bible references to the source of the *Problem of Evil*, and mention extreme examples quoted in contradiction.
5. Explain the reasons given in the text for God's permission of evil.
6. Cite Job and Saint Paul in defence of this explanation and state the "most likely reason for the fact of evil" given in the text.
7. Show how death itself gives a clue as to the compatibility of evil and God's goodness and develop this idea quoting (approximately) Saint Peter and Saint Paul.
8. Elaborate the sentence: "The torrent of proof (as to the heritage of sin) contained in the means of our salvation by the suffering voluntarily accepted by God Himself for our sake, should remove any lingering doubt in the mind of man."
9. How does Christ invite us to share in the glory won by His Sacrifice?
10. Narrate the author's "brush with the problem of evil" and his final admonition for prayer.

CHAPTER XVII

DEATH — THE GOAL OF LIFE

The traditional missionary of old rarely ended his preaching without an heroic effort to chill the marrow in the bones of his hearers by a description of hell so vivid and horrible, and a description of the suffering of the souls in Purgatory so heart-rending and so full of the sense of physical pain that the young ones might have bad dreams and the older ones would be gravely moved. The idea was, of course, to sound a warning which would deter souls from their evil deeds — to *drive* them away from all wicked temptations and occasions of sin by attempting to awaken in them a perennial fear of hell. Alas, however, the result has too often been to give them nothing but a half-subconscious and unexamined fear of death.

Now, far be it from any Catholic priest to give the impression of discounting the pains of hell, or of giving the slightest support to the common modern notion that the very definite word of Christ: "Begone from me you accursed, into everlasting fire which is prepared for the devil and his angels! " (Mat. 25:41). — is only a "symbolic" invitation to follow the Golden Rule. This notion is especially to be disowned by every Catholic priest or layman when the word "symbolic" is understood in the sense I have mentioned in a previous chapter as: "Pictorial expressions of spiritual truths, even though the supposed facts themselves did not actually happen." (Doct. p. 37).[1]

The result of all this has been that during the past fifty years, nearly all religion except the Catholic Faith has consigned all the negative urge toward goodness as exemplified by the fear of hell, to the convenient category of symbolism and so has comfortably closed the gates of hell.

But while this has been a means of destroying a most forceful sanction of the moral law in the hearts of sensual men, the voice of conscience which God has placed by nature in every soul, is not so easily disowned. The net result is that the salutary fear of hell has been replaced by a nebulous and unreasoned fear of death, to which most men respond by putting it out of their minds with the same vigor which should be employed in flying from evil thoughts.

This attitude toward hell and death has become so prevalent and so convenient that far too many Catholics have become contaminated with it. While they do not actually deny the fact of hell and eternal punishment for the wicked, they allow the behavior of others to dim their own advertence to its reality and end by having a cordial fear of death which causes them to suppress all thought of it and all mention of it for themselves or for their dear ones to the point of tragic danger to their salvation.

The shocking truth is, as I have learned to my amazement, that doctors find that it is usually dangerous to inform their patients that death is near unless the symptoms are such as to make it obvious to the patient himself. When the X-Ray picture in the hands of a cancer specialist caused him to tell me that, barring a miracle, my wife could not be expected to live more than three

---

1. Doctrine In The Church Of England. The report of the Commission on Christian Doctrine appointed by Archbishops of Canterbury and York in 1922.

months, he advised me to think up some excuse to explain why he had cancelled the order for an immediate operation. When I insisted that the only possible explanation was the truth, he refused to have any part of the responsibility. True, he was not a Catholic and did not know how a Catholic should be prepared for death, but that anyone should have such a fear of death, is a tragic commentary on present day psychology. This dangerous psychology takes various forms, but to the great regret of every priest, it too often manifests itself by a reluctance to ask for the Last Sacraments until too late for their efficacy.

It is a blessing that in 1973 the Holy See has taken steps to relieve this situation. The Sacrament is now to be called *the Anointing of the Sick* and is worded so that it "relieves and strengthens the soul of the sick person, arousing in him a great confidence in the divine mercy." (L'O.Rom. Feb. 1, 1973).

Now, every Catholic knows, or should know, that hell is just as real as his own flesh and bones. He also knows that it is something to be dreaded, *only* as a punishment for unrepented grave sin. He knows that he should think of hell when he is tempted to commit sin. He knows that he will go to hell if he is guilty of grave sin and unrepentant at the time of his death. It will therefore be his own fault. While he knows that we do not understand fully the nature of the punishment of hell, he also knows that it is to be dreaded beyond the possibility of comparison with sense pain alone. He knows that our nearest approach to appreciation of the vigor with which hell should be hated, comes when we add to its positive pains, the pain of loss of the eternal joy of heaven, which is equally beyond the grasp of our understanding, but of which St. Paul reminds us that: "Eye hath not seen nor ear heard, nor hath it entered into the heart of man to conceive what God has prepared for those that love Him." (I Cor. 2:9). And St. Thomas Aquinas describes it as: "That ineffable banquet, where Thou, with Thy Son and the Holy Spirit, art to Thy saints true light, fullness of content, eternal joy, gladness without alloy and perfect bliss."

While he knows that our fallen human nature is too fickle to be given any certain guarantee of final perseverance in a state of grace at the hour of death, he also knows that God, who loves him more than he can possibly love God, has planned it that way as a salutary stimulus to seek God alone, and not as a threat to invite despair. He knows that God, our loving Father, has revealed to us the truth about hell to make us dread sin, not to make us dread death.

He knows, for example, that the admonition contained in the Holy Rule of St. Benedict – that a Monk as well as every Christian, should "keep death daily before his eyes," is not intended to make life an uneasy struggle, but rather it is to remind him that our whole life from beginning to end has for its purpose in the scheme of creation, our happy entry into heaven, and that every minute of every day that life lasts is the "acceptable time" to prepare for the day of salvation which, for each one of us, is the day of our death.

He knows that all our merits accumulate before God and are always in His sight. In other words, to have death daily before one's eyes was never suggested by St. Benedict to cause his Monks to seek a negative and pessimistic approach to salvation in cowering fear before a vindictive God of justice.

On the contrary, such a motive is inconsistent with the whole atmosphere of Christian life reflected in St. Benedict's Rule, which is typically expressed in the Prologue, quoting Psalm 33: "Who is the man who will have life and desireth to see good days?" – "and if thou hearing him answer, 'I am he,' God saith to thee: 'If thou wilt have true and everlasting life, keep thy tongue from evil and thy lips that they speak no guile. Turn from evil and

do good: seek peace and pursue it.' " (cf. Ps. 33:13-15).
"And when you have done these things, My eyes will be
upon you, and My ears will be open to your prayer; and
before you call upon Me, I will say to you, 'Behold I am
here.' What can be sweeter to us, dearest brethren, than
this voice of the Lord inviting us? Behold in His loving
kindness the Lord showeth unto us the way of life."
(Prologue of Holy Rule).

St. Benedict then continues in a manner quite consistent with his salutary admonition to be always mindful
of death as a goal toward which life is directed. He says:
"As we go forward in our life and in faith, we shall, with
hearts enlarged and with unspeakable sweetness of love,
run in the way of God's commandments; so that never
departing from His guidance, but persevering in His teaching in the Monastery until death, we may deserve to be
partakers of His Kingdom."

I wish with all my heart to second St. Benedict's
invitation to keep death daily before our eyes, but the
approach which I recommend, while not wishing to
obscure the salutary fear of hell, looks upon the hour of
death as a goal which we are approaching with faith,
hope, and charity — and not as a calamity which is approaching us in company with fear, hate and severity.

In short, the incentive to be good for the love of God
is far more effective in time of temptation than is the
negative deterrent of fear, especially in this day and age
when the fear of hell has lost most of its followers outside the Catholic Church. Furthermore, it gives far more
purpose to all that we do hour by hour and day by day.
The only motive worth its salt for every thought and
word and act stems from the fact that one believes with
all his heart that Jesus Christ is God — he loves Him for
the length He has gone to for his Redemption, and he
wants to show Christ his love in everything he does. But
this very motive is given point when it is remembered
that the loving Christ always has your whole life in view

while you, like a little child, are busily working before His eyes, always putting your pennies in the little bank while He looks on with loving approval.

And what are these pennies we are accumulating? They are the coin we *can* take with us when we die – merit – grace – and "promisory notes of heavenly glory." Here and now, they are earned by prayer and good works and the Sacraments. The wonderful thing about this pay is that it can be enjoyed while it is being hoarded. The soul hoarding merit and grace against the hour of death, experiences peace and joy which is never even dreamed of by the unbeliever who is, so to say, living from hand-to-mouth in a sort of spiritual merry-go-round, trying to forget that *this* part of the performance will come to an abrupt end rather soon. Secretly, perhaps, for good manners, but none the less safely, the believer can laugh with pity at this unbeliever who ridicules his practice of virtue with the taunt: "Eat, drink and be merry! You can't take it with you when you die! " The reason there is value to the treasure he is hoarding is precisely because you *can* take it with you when you die!

And this brings up a point that many Catholics and more non-Catholics do not realize: The extent of our everlasting enjoyment of the vision of God in heaven is determined, not by the mere fact that we find the "gate" open or shut when we come to die; on the contrary: "When the Son of Man comes in His glory with His angels about Him, then will He reward every man *according to his works*." (Matt. 16:27).

Every thought and word and act of our lives has bearing on our enjoyment of heaven. Those which conform to the will of God will increase our heavenly reward; those contrary to the will of God will decrease it – even if they do not cause our exclusion from heaven. Exactly *how* this is true, we cannot know in this world, for the very reason that "it has not entered into the heart of man to conceive what God has prepared for them that love Him." Christ, however, has left no doubt *that* it is true.

If one enters whole-heartedly into this hopeful teaching of Christ, it is easy to see how the everlasting value of every minute can add tremendous importance to everything we do and can not only take away the sting of approaching death, but can really make it a goal to be sought with joy.

For myself, since God in His mercy has given me the most precious gift obtainable in this world, the gift of the holy priesthood, I look forward to the day of my death as the happiest day left for me in this world. I say this, not with presumption, but rather in the foot-steps of St. Paul, who learned it directly from Christ. In other words — if my faith means anything at all, it means that: "To live is Christ, and to die is gain! If it be my lot to go on living in the flesh, this will be fruitful of labor for me; and so I know not which to choose, but I am hard pressed between the two, having the desire to depart and to be with Christ, for this is far better; yet to remain in the flesh may be needful to conform to His will." (cf. Phil. 1:21-24).

And that is all I need to know! To profess any other attitude toward life and death is, I believe, a confession of grave deficiency of the essential virtues of Faith and Hope.

I believe with all my heart that Jesus Christ is God. I believe that He died for my salvation. I believe that if I fail to share in that salvation, it will be my own fault. I am aware that no man can have absolute certainty of his state of grace at any time; still less does he have any guarantee of final perseverance at the hour of death. But I mean to try with all my might to spend all the time between now and the hour of my death to make that hour welcome. I believe that Christ loves me even though I am weak, and I trust Him to give me the grace to please Him always, even at the hour of death.

I know that the hour of death may be the hour of greatest trial in this life, but I also know that, "as a man lives, so shall he die." And so I have a right to hope without presumption that Christ who loves me, will give me the grace to die loving Him.

Not only do I believe and hope as I have said, but I would be ashamed to admit that my faith does not confirm the belief that everything I do between now and the hour of death will add to, or detract from the talent which Christ has given me to trade with until He returns at the hour of my death.

Christ said: "Whoever gives to one of these little ones a cup of cold water to drink because he is a disciple, indeed I tell you he shall by no means lose his reward." (Matt. 10:42). I believe that, and so I say: – "What is the use of spending any of the time Christ has given us in any other way than in trying to qualify for that reward?"

So – let us return to the question which has already suggested itself: – "How does one go about trading with his talent of grace to build up his treasure in heaven?" This we have already answered in part: – By the Sacraments, by prayer and by good works. Now, the Sacraments are the unique and most prolific channels of grace and heavenly treasure, but each Sacrament is also a most efficacious prayer and also a good work; and every good work with the right intention, is a prayer; and so too, every prayer is a good work. So, it is easy to see that all these means have much in common. But let us look at some of the special virtues of each.

First and foremost, for one who has been freed from sin and so placed in a state of sanctifying grace – the Blessed Sacrament of Christ's Body and Blood is the most efficacious means of storing up treasure in heaven. Not only does it of itself give us a tremendous increase of grace, but it places the very Source of grace in our hearts and so gives added merit to everything else we try to do. And so, to celebrate or assist at Mass and receive Communion, is by all odds the very most profitable way to spend one's time, provided, of course, that it does not interfere with other things we are bound to do under obedience to the will of God. To tie it to the point in hand, of daily preparation for the hour of death, let us recall that beautiful little Communion Hymn:

> O Sacred Banquet, in which Christ is received,
> The memory of His Passion is recalled,
> The mind is filled with grace,
> And there is given to us a pledge of future glory.

Here we are reminded of the adage: — "As the Church prays, so does she teach." And so we believe that in receiving the Body and Blood of Christ in Holy Communion, we receive with it a pledge of future glory which is redeemable if we continue to cooperate with grace.

Very precious also is the Sacrament of Penance, or, if one has had the misfortune to fall from a state of grace, it is an infinite treasure. And, as applied to the day-by-day preparation for the hour of death, we should never lose sight of the two-fold virtue of the Sacrament of Penance. Not only does it erase the guilt of past sin, provided it is honestly regretted with a firm purpose of amendment, but it fortifies the soul for the future with priceless Sacramental Grace that increases the efficacy of our other good works and strengthens our resistance to temptation.

And the same is true in some degree of each of the other Sacraments. Each has its special sacramental grace to equip us for our state in life and to give us strength to prepare for the hour of death with greater assurance. Baptism brings first Sanctifying Grace and admits to all the other Sacraments. Confirmation, as the name implies, gives added strength to meet added trials. Marriage and Holy Orders provide special graces for special states of life. The Last Anointing is above all *the* Sacrament of fortification for the hour of death. It should be sought by every soul if and whenever he is in danger of death.

All prayer should have at least a secondary purpose of gaining treasure in heaven. Every soul who wishes to do the will of God is preparing for death when he prays with faith – from the tiny non-Catholic child who prays: "If I should die before I wake, I pray Thee, Lord, my soul to take" – to the Catholic who seeks all life long to solicit the intercession of the Blessed Virgin when he prays: "Pray for us sinners now, and at the hour of our death! "

And so, in everything we do, if we practice the Benedictine motto: "Let God be glorified in all things," we may and should await with peace and joy and confidence the gracious call from God at the hour and in the manner which He has ordained for every living soul! Above all, let us resolve that we will never lose sight of that purpose of our lives of which we are reminded whenever a priest sings the Preface of the Mass of Requiem for the dead: "For unto Thy faithful, O Lord, life is changed, not taken away, and the abode of this earthly sojourn being dissolved, an eternal dwelling place is prepared in heaven."

Study Questions:

1. Explain the old form of deterrent from sin through fear of hell and show its inefficacy as a result of the "closing of the Gates of Hell."

2. Tell how the fear of death has replaced the fear of hell and describe the author's experience with this problem.

3. State the true Catholic answer to this problem.

4. Show how a "cowering fear before a vindictive God of justice is inconsistent with the whole atmosphere of Christian life." (quoting, approximately, St. Benedict's Rule).

5. Cite the author's recommendation of St. Benedict's invitation to "keep death daily before our eyes," and elaborate this idea.

6. Elaborate the notion of the "penny bank" we *can* take with

us when we die and comment on the *degree* of beatitude
available.

7. Cite the author's comment on the approach of his own death.

8. Elaborate the answer to the question: "How does one go
about trading with his talent of grace to build up his treasure
in heaven? "

9. Discuss the special merits of the Sacraments of Penance and
the Eucharist for treasure in heaven and refer the latter to the
Communion Hymn quoted in the text.

10. Give a fitting conclusion to the chapter on *Death – the Goal
of Life.*